Better Homes and Gardens®
all-time favorites

Better Homes and Gardens® Books
Des Moines, Iowa

Better Homes and Gardens® Books
An imprint of Meredith® Books

All-Time Favorites

Project Editors: Spectrum Communication Services, Inc.

Project Designers: Conyers Design Collaborative, Inc.

Copy Chief: Catherine Hamrick

Copy and Production Editor: Terri Fredrickson

Contributing Copy Editor: Jennifer Speer Ramundt

Contributing Proofreaders: Gretchen Kauffman, Susan J. Kling

Electronic Production Coordinator: Paula Forest

Editorial and Design Assistants: Judy Bailey, Mary Lee Gavin, Karen Schirm

Test Kitchen Director: Lynn Blanchard

Production Director: Douglas M. Johnston

Production Managers: Pam Kvitne, Marjorie J. Schenkelberg

Meredith® Books

Editor in Chief: James D. Blume

Design Director: Matt Strelecki

Managing Editor: Gregory H. Kayko

Director, Sales & Marketing, Retail: Michael A. Peterson

Director, Sales & Marketing, Special Markets: Rita McMullen

Director, Sales & Marketing, Home & Garden Center Channel: Ray Wolf

Director, Operations: George A. Susral

Vice President, General Manager: Jamie L. Martin

Better Homes and Gardens® Magazine

Editor in Chief: Jean LemMon

Executive Food Editor: Nancy Byal

Meredith Publishing Group

President, Publishing Group: Christopher M. Little

Vice President, Consumer Marketing & Development: Hal Oringer

Meredith Corporation

Chairman and Chief Executive Officer: William T. Kerr

Chairman of the Executive Committee: E. T. Meredith III

All of us at Better Homes and Gardens® Books are dedicated to providing you with the information and ideas you need to create delicious foods. We welcome your comments and suggestions. Write to us at: Better Homes and Gardens Books, Cookbook Editorial Department, 1716 Locust St. Des Moines, Iowa 50309-3023.

Our seal assures you that every recipe in *All-Time Favorites* has been tested in the Better Homes and Gardens® Test Kitchen. This means that each recipe is practical and reliable, and meets our high standards of taste appeal. We guarantee your satisfaction with this book for as long as you own it.

Better Homes and Gardens. all-time favorites

Contents

Better Homes and Gardens.
all-time favorites

"This book is your starting point for a whole new adventure in meal making," wrote the editors of *My Better Homes and Gardens Cook Book* in 1930, the first edition of what is now known as *Better Homes and Gardens New Cook Book.* For generations, millions of cooks have relied on this red plaid cookbook as they would a trusted friend. To capture the best of the 70 years of cooking reflected in this classic, we have created *All-Time Favorites.* Thumb through the pages of this special volume, and you'll find page-after-page of time-honored recipes, all pulled from the 11 editions of the *Better Homes and Gardens® New Cook Book.*

Better Homes and Gardens® Books food editors have always insisted on quality and accuracy. In fact, in 1930 they exhorted readers to "measure accurately, and to follow directions for mixing, handling, time, and temperature." To ensure continued quality and guarantee success using today's modern appliances, all the recipes in *All-Time Favorites* have been tested and updated in the Better Homes and Gardens® Test Kitchen. Modifications were kept to a minimum, however, in order to retain the tried-and-true tastes of the originals.

We hope you'll savor these heirloom recipes, snippets of history, and nostalgic illustrations. It's a peek into the past that we think you'll treasure for a lifetime.

snacks & beverages

Cheese balls and dips came into their own during the 1950s, and our first cheese ball recipe appeared in the 1953 edition. This recipe, however, hails from the early 1980s and features a tongue-tingling blend of smoky cheddar cheese, steak sauce, and cream cheese rolled in nuts.

1981 Smoky Cheese Ball

Prep: 35 minutes   Chill: 4 to 24 hours

2 **8-ounce packages cream cheese**	2 **tablespoons milk**
2 **cups shredded smoked cheddar, Swiss, or Gouda cheese**	2 **teaspoons steak sauce**
½ **cup margarine or butter, softened**	1 **cup finely chopped nuts, toasted** **Assorted crackers**

Bring cheeses and margarine or butter to room temperature. Add milk and steak sauce; beat with electric mixer until fluffy. Cover; chill in refrigerator for at least 4 hours or up to 24 hours. Shape mixture into ball. Roll in nuts. Let stand for 15 minutes. Serve with crackers. Makes 3½ cups spread.

Nutrition facts per tablespoon spread: 74 calories, **7 g** total fat (**3 g** saturated fat), **13 mg** cholesterol, **72 mg** sodium, **1 g** carbohydrate, **0 g** fiber, **2 g** protein

Enthusiasm for Mexican dining was just starting to spread to the rest of the country from the southwestern United States in the 1950s. So our first version of this recipe was a rather novel adaptation based on a can of pork and beans. American palates have become more sophisticated about Mexican food since then, and our current recipe is much closer to the traditional classic.

1953 Chili con Queso

Start to finish: 30 minutes

½ **cup finely chopped onion (1 medium)**	1 **cup shredded American cheese (4 ounces)**
1 **tablespoon margarine or butter**	1 **cup shredded Monterey Jack cheese (4 ounces)**
1⅓ **cups chopped, seeded tomatoes (2 medium)**	1 **teaspoon cornstarch**
1 **4-ounce can diced green chili peppers, drained**	1 **teaspoon bottled hot pepper sauce** **Tortilla or corn chips**

In a saucepan cook onion in margarine or butter until tender. Stir in tomatoes and chili peppers. Simmer, uncovered, for 10 minutes.

Toss cheeses with cornstarch. Gradually add cheese mixture to saucepan, stirring until melted. Stir in hot pepper sauce; heat through. Serve with chips. Makes 1¾ cups dip.

Nutrition facts per tablespoon dip: 35 calories, **3 g** total fat (**1 g** saturated fat), **6 mg** cholesterol, **94 mg** sodium, **1 g** carbohydrate, **0 g** fiber, **2 g** protein

Crunchy Party Mix

Prep: 15 minutes   Bake: 45 minutes

1 **cup margarine or butter**	4 **cups round toasted oat cereal**
3 **tablespoons Worcestershire sauce**	4 **cups bite-size wheat or bran square cereal**
½ **teaspoon garlic powder**	4 **cups bite-size rice or corn square cereal**
Several drops bottled hot pepper sauce	**or bite-size shredded wheat biscuits**
5 **cups tiny pretzels or pretzel sticks**	3 **cups mixed nuts**

Heat and stir margarine or butter, Worcestershire sauce, garlic powder, and hot pepper sauce until margarine melts. In a large roasting pan combine pretzels, cereals, and nuts. Drizzle margarine mixture over cereal mixture; toss to coat.

Bake in a 300° oven for 45 minutes, stirring every 15 minutes. Spread on foil; cool. Store in an airtight container. Makes 20 cups.

Nutrition facts per ½ cup: 165 calories, **11 g** total fat (**2 g** saturated fat), **0 mg** cholesterol, **237 mg** sodium, **14 g** carbohydrate, **2 g** fiber, **3 g** protein

In the 1970s and early 1980s, someone was sure to bring to parties a snack mix based on bite-size wheat, rice, corn, or bran cereal. This zesty recipe was our version of the fad.

Hot Spiced Cider

Prep: 10 minutes   Cook: 10 minutes

8 **cups apple cider or apple juice**	1 **teaspoon whole allspice**
¼ **to ½ cup packed brown sugar**	1 **teaspoon whole cloves**
6 **inches stick cinnamon**	8 **thin orange wedges (optional)**
	8 **whole cloves (optional)**

In a saucepan combine cider and brown sugar. For spice bag, place cinnamon, allspice, and the 1 teaspoon whole cloves on a double-thick, 6-inch-square piece of 100% cotton cheesecloth. Bring corners together and tie with a clean string. Add bag to cider mixture.

Bring to boiling; reduce heat. Cover and simmer for 10 minutes. Meanwhile, if desired, stud orange wedges with the 8 cloves. Remove spice bag; discard. Serve cider in mugs. If desired, put a clove-studded orange wedge in each mug. Makes 8 (about 8-ounce) servings.

Nutrition facts per serving: 145 calories, **0 g** total fat, **0 mg** cholesterol, **9 mg** sodium, **40 g** carbohydrate, **0 g** fiber, **0 g** protein

Dubbed Hot Mulled Cider in 1953, this fragrant, fruity blend was the perfect antidote to the winter chills. Follow the example of those 1950s' hostesses and hosts and serve this smooth sipper at holiday parties. Or, put some in a thermos and tote it along to a tailgate party or an after-ski gathering.

In our 1981 cookbook, this punch (without the wine) was an all-purpose base to which you could add wine, hard liquor, or lemon-lime carbonated beverage. Today, we feature it with dry white wine. For a nonalcoholic version, you can substitute two 1-liter bottles of chilled club soda or carbonated water for the wine.

1981 Spiced Fruit Punch
Prep: 15 minutes   Cook: 10 minutes   Chill: 2 to 24 hours

½ **cup water**	1 **12-ounce can apricot**
⅓ **cup sugar**	**nectar, chilled**
12 **inches stick cinnamon,**	¼ **cup lemon juice**
broken	2 **750-milliliter bottles**
½ **teaspoon whole cloves**	**dry white wine,**
4 **cups apple cider or**	**chilled**
apple juice, chilled	**Orange slices,**
	quartered (optional)

In a saucepan combine water, sugar, and spices. Bring to boiling; reduce heat. Cover and simmer for 10 minutes. Cover and chill in refrigerator for at least 2 hours or up to 24 hours.

Strain spices from sugar-water and discard. Combine the sugar-water and fruit juices. Pour into punch bowl; add wine. If desired, garnish with quartered orange slices. Makes 24 (about 4-ounce) servings.

Nutrition facts per serving: 81 calories, **0 g** total fat, **0 mg** cholesterol, **5 mg** sodium, **10 g** carbohydrate, **0 g** fiber, **0 g** protein

Eggnog
Prep: 15 minutes   Cook: 10 minutes   Chill: 4 to 24 hours

6	beaten egg yolks	1	to 3 tablespoons bourbon
2	cups milk	1	teaspoon vanilla
⅓	cup sugar	1	cup whipping cream
1	to 3 tablespoons light rum	2	tablespoons sugar Ground nutmeg

In a large heavy saucepan mix the egg yolks, milk, and the ⅓ cup sugar. Cook and stir over medium heat until mixture just coats a metal spoon. Remove from heat. Place the pan in a sink or bowl of ice water and stir for 2 minutes. Stir in rum, bourbon, and vanilla. Cover and chill in the refrigerator for at least 4 hours or up to 24 hours.

Just before serving, in a mixing bowl beat the whipping cream and the 2 tablespoons sugar until soft peaks form. Transfer chilled egg mixture to a punch bowl. Fold in the whipped cream mixture. Serve immediately. Sprinkle each serving with nutmeg. Makes 10 (about 4-ounce) servings.

Chocolate Eggnog: Prepare as above, except stir ¼ to ⅓ cup chocolate-flavored syrup into egg mixture before chilling.

Nonalcoholic Eggnog: Prepare as above, except omit the rum and bourbon. Increase the milk to 2¼ to 2½ cups.

Nutrition facts per serving: 201 calories, **13 g** total fat (**7 g** saturated fat), **164 mg** cholesterol, **71 mg** sodium, **13 g** carbohydrate, **0 g** fiber, **6 g** protein
   Nutrition facts per serving for Chocolate Eggnog: 211 calories, **13 g** total fat (**7 g** saturated fat)
   Nutrition facts per serving for Nonalcoholic Eggnog: 191 calories, **13 g** total fat (**7 g** saturated fat)

The eggnog of 1930 was simply an egg mixed with milk, some sugar, and a little vanilla, rather than the thick, creamy, custard-based libation of our current edition.

Glazed Nuts
(see recipe, below),
Divinity (see recipe,
opposite page),
and Old-Time Fudge
(see recipe, page 12)

Glazed almonds were a favorite treat in the late 1960s because they didn't require a candy thermometer and were less work than making nut brittle. That's true today, too— except we've expanded the technique to cover cashews, peanuts, and pecans.

Glazed Nuts

Prep: 5 minutes   Cook: 6 minutes   Cool: 45 minutes

1½ **cups blanched whole almonds, raw cashews, raw peanuts, or pecan halves**	½ **cup sugar** 2 **tablespoons butter or margarine** **Salt (optional)**

In a heavy 8-inch skillet combine nuts, sugar, and butter or margarine. Cook over medium heat, stirring constantly with wooden spoon, for 6 to 8 minutes or until sugar is melted and golden in color and nuts are toasted. Spread nuts on a buttered, foil-lined baking sheet. If desired, sprinkle lightly with salt. Cool. Separate into clusters. Makes about ¾ pound.

Nutrition facts per ounce: 145 calories, **10 g** total fat (**2 g** saturated fat), **5 mg** cholesterol, **21 mg** sodium, **12 g** carbohydrate, **1 g** fiber, **3 g** protein

 **Divinity**
Prep: 25 minutes   Cook: 10 minutes

2½ cups sugar
 ½ cup light-colored corn
     syrup
 ½ cup water
 2 egg whites

1 teaspoon vanilla
1 or 2 drops food coloring
    (optional)
½ cup chopped candied
    fruit and/or nuts

In a heavy 2-quart saucepan combine sugar, corn syrup, and water. Cook and stir over medium-high heat until mixture boils. Clip a candy thermometer to the side of the pan. Reduce heat to medium; continue cooking, without stirring, until the thermometer registers 260°, hard-ball stage (10 to 15 minutes).

Remove saucepan from heat; remove thermometer. In a large mixing bowl beat egg whites with a freestanding electric mixer on medium speed until stiff peaks form (tips stand straight). Gradually pour hot mixture in a thin stream over egg whites, beating on high speed about 3 minutes; scrape side of bowl occasionally. Add vanilla and, if desired, food coloring. Continue beating on high speed just until candy starts to lose its gloss (5 to 6 minutes). When beaters are lifted, mixture should fall in a ribbon that mounds on itself.

Drop a spoonful of candy mixture onto waxed paper. If it stays mounded, the mixture has been beaten sufficiently. If mixture flattens, beat ½ to 1 minute more; check again. If mixture is too stiff to spoon, beat in a few drops hot water until candy is a softer consistency. Immediately stir in fruit and/or nuts. Quickly drop mixture onto waxed paper. Store tightly covered. Makes about 40 pieces.

Nutrition facts per piece: 66 calories, **0 g** total fat, **0 mg** cholesterol, **6 mg** sodium, **17 g** carbohydrate, **0 g** fiber, **0 g** protein

In 1930 we instructed readers how to make a divinity roll filled with a mixture of raisins, dates, figs, and nuts. By 1937, however, our recipe for divinity turned out the standard mounds of fluff that candy lovers know today.

In the days before the marshmallow creme version, beating fudge by hand was the only way to make the irresistible confection. Today, many purists still feel the texture of traditional fudge is worth the extra effort.

Old-Time Fudge
Prep: 20 minutes   Cook: 20 minutes   Cool: 55 minutes

2 **cups sugar**	2 **tablespoons butter**
¾ **cup milk**	1 **teaspoon vanilla**
2 **ounces unsweetened chocolate, cut up**	½ **cup chopped nuts (optional)**
1 **teaspoon light-colored corn syrup**	**Walnut halves (optional)**

Line a 9×5×3-inch loaf pan with foil, extending foil over edges of pan. Butter foil; set pan aside.

Butter the side of a heavy 2-quart saucepan. In saucepan combine sugar, milk, chocolate, and corn syrup. Cook and stir over medium-high heat until mixture boils. Clip a candy thermometer to side of pan. Reduce heat to medium-low; continue boiling at a moderate, steady rate, stirring frequently, until thermometer registers 234°, soft-ball stage (20 to 25 minutes).

Remove saucepan from heat. Add butter and vanilla, but do not stir. Cool, without stirring, to 110° (about 55 minutes).

Remove thermometer from saucepan. Beat mixture vigorously with a wooden spoon until fudge just begins to thicken. If desired, add chopped nuts. Continue beating until the fudge becomes very thick and just starts to lose its gloss (about 10 minutes).

Immediately spread fudge in the prepared pan. Score into squares while warm. When fudge is firm, use foil to lift it out of pan. Cut fudge into squares. If desired, garnish with walnut halves. Store fudge tightly covered. Makes about 1¼ pounds (32 pieces).

Nutrition facts per piece: 67 calories, **2 g** total fat (**1 g** saturated fat), **2 mg** cholesterol, **11 mg** sodium, **14 g** carbohydrate, **0 g** fiber, **0 g** protein

main dishes

 Swiss Steak
Prep: 25 minutes
Cook: 1¼ hours

1	pound boneless beef round steak, cut ¾ inch thick
2	tablespoons all-purpose flour
¼	teaspoon salt
¼	teaspoon pepper
1	tablespoon cooking oil
1	16-ounce can tomatoes, cut up
1	small onion, sliced and separated into rings
½	cup sliced celery (1 stalk)
½	cup sliced carrot (1 medium)
½	teaspoon dried thyme, crushed
2	cups hot cooked rice or noodles

Our first Swiss Steak recipe appeared in the late 1930s and was seasoned only with a little salt, pepper, onion, and mustard. Over the years, the ingredients have changed to include more flavorful items, such as tomatoes, celery, and carrot. With today's recipe you can take your choice of range-top, oven, or crockery cooker methods.

Trim fat from meat. Cut into 4 serving-size pieces. Combine the flour, salt, and pepper. With the notched side of a meat mallet, pound flour mixture into meat.

In a large skillet brown meat on both sides in hot oil. Drain off fat. Add undrained tomatoes, onion, celery, carrot, and thyme. Bring to boiling; reduce heat. Cover and simmer about 1¼ hours or until meat is tender. Skim off fat. Serve with rice or noodles. Makes 4 servings.

Oven directions: Prepare and brown meat in skillet as above. Transfer meat to a 2-quart square baking dish. In the same skillet combine undrained tomatoes, onion, celery, carrot, and thyme. Bring to boiling, scraping up any browned bits. Pour over meat. Cover and bake in a 350° oven about 1 hour or until tender. Serve as above.

Crockery-cooker directions: Trim fat from meat. Cut into 4 serving-size pieces. Omit flouring and pounding meat. Brown meat in hot oil. In a 3½- or 4-quart electric crockery cooker place onion, celery, and carrot. Sprinkle with thyme, 2 tablespoons quick-cooking tapioca, salt, and pepper. Pour undrained tomatoes over vegetables. Add meat. Cover and cook on low-heat setting for 10 to 12 hours. Serve as above.

Nutrition facts per serving: 352 calories, **9 g** total fat (**2 g** saturated fat), **72 mg** cholesterol, **404 mg** sodium, **34 g** carbohydrate, **2 g** fiber, **31 g** protein

Lemon Sirloin Steak

Prep: 20 minutes   Marinate: 2 to 6 hours   Grill: 16 minutes

1 **boneless beef sirloin steak, cut 1½ inches thick (2 to 2½ pounds)**	⅔ **cup lemon juice**
	⅓ **cup cooking oil**
2 **green onions, thinly sliced (¼ cup)**	1 **tablespoon Worcestershire sauce**
1 **teaspoon finely shredded lemon peel**	1 **tablespoon prepared mustard**
	½ **teaspoon salt**
	¼ **teaspoon pepper**

Trim fat from meat. Place meat in plastic bag set in shallow dish. For marinade, combine remaining ingredients; pour over meat. Close bag. Marinate meat for 2 to 6 hours in refrigerator, turning the bag occasionally.

Remove meat from marinade; pat dry. Grill on rack of uncovered grill directly over medium coals, turning over halfway through grilling time. (Allow 16 to 18 minutes for medium-rare or 18 to 22 minutes for medium doneness.) Brush occasionally with marinade up to the last 5 minutes of cooking. To serve, thinly slice across grain. Serves 8 to 10.

Nutrition facts per serving: 246 calories, **15 g** total fat (**5 g** saturated fat), **76 mg** cholesterol, **144 mg** sodium, **1 g** carbohydrate, **0 g** fiber, **26 g** protein

Cooks generally marinate meat for tenderness, flavor, or both. In this case, since sirloin steak is usually tender enough, this marinade is used simply for the delicious flavor it imparts. Two hours of marinating delivers a hint of tangy lemon, while a full six-hour marinade makes this dish sing of citrus.

Hungarian Goulash

Prep: 20 minutes   Cook: 1 hour

2½ **pounds beef or veal round steak, cut into ½-inch cubes**	¾ **teaspoon dried thyme, crushed**
¼ **cup cooking oil**	1 **28-ounce can tomatoes, cut up**
1 **cup chopped onion**	2 **bay leaves**
1 **clove garlic, minced**	1 **8-ounce carton dairy sour cream**
¼ **cup all-purpose flour**	4 **cups hot cooked noodles**
4 **teaspoons paprika**	

In large saucepan or Dutch oven brown meat, half at a time, in hot oil, cooking onion and garlic with second batch of meat. Drain off fat. Return all of meat to pan. Stir in flour, paprika, thyme, ½ teaspoon salt, and ¼ teaspoon pepper. Add undrained tomatoes and bay leaves. Bring to boiling; reduce heat. Cover and simmer for 1 to 1¼ hours for beef (50 to 60 minutes for veal) or until meat is tender. Discard bay leaves. Stir in sour cream. Heat through; do not boil. Serve over noodles. Makes 8 servings.

Nutrition facts per serving: 440 calories, **17 g** total fat (**7 g** saturated fat), **128 mg** cholesterol, **378 mg** sodium, **29 g** carbohydrate, **3 g** fiber, **40 g** protein

Paprika is a key ingredient in many recipes of Hungarian origin. This powder, ground from dried, mild, red chili peppers, adds a special flavor that varies from sweet to hot. But the story doesn't end with the flavor. Many times paprika is used solely for the beautiful red hue it bestows.

Seasoned cornmeal over a spicy mélange of shredded beef, tomatoes, onions, and olives creates a one-dish meal that smells so good as it bakes, your patience will be stretched to the limit. But once it's out of the oven and the flavor fiesta has begun, your only thought will be when you can make it again.

 Tamale Pie
1946 Prep: 35 minutes   Bake: 25 minutes   Stand: 5 minutes

2 **medium onions, chopped**	¼ **teaspoon salt**
3 **cloves garlic, minced**	3 **cups shredded, cooked roast beef (12 ounces)**
2 **tablespoons cooking oil**	1¼ **cups yellow cornmeal**
1 **28-ounce can tomatoes, cut up**	1 **cup cold water**
2 **2¼-ounce cans sliced pitted ripe olives**	2 **cups water**
½ **cup raisins (optional)**	½ **teaspoon salt**
2 **tablespoons chili powder**	½ **teaspoon chili powder**
	1 **cup shredded American or cheddar cheese (4 ounces)**

In a large saucepan cook onion and garlic in hot oil until tender. Drain off fat. Stir in the undrained tomatoes, olives, raisins (if using), the 2 tablespoons chili powder, and the ¼ teaspoon salt. Bring to boiling; reduce heat. Simmer, uncovered, about 20 minutes or until slightly thickened. Stir in cooked beef; heat through. Spread beef mixture evenly into an ungreased 3-quart rectangular baking dish; set aside.

Meanwhile, combine cornmeal and the 1 cup cold water. Set aside. In a medium saucepan bring the 2 cups water to boiling; add the ½ teaspoon salt and ½ teaspoon chili powder. Slowly add cornmeal mixture to boiling water, stirring constantly. Return to boiling, stirring constantly. Reduce heat to low. Cook for 10 to 15 minutes or until mixture is very thick, stirring occasionally. Spread the cornmeal mixture evenly over beef mixture.

Bake in a 325° oven for 20 minutes. Sprinkle with cheese. Bake for 5 minutes more. Let stand 5 minutes before serving. Makes 6 to 8 servings.

Nutrition facts per serving: 424 calories, **22 g total** fat (**7 g** saturated fat), **69 mg** cholesterol, **958 mg** sodium, **33 g** carbohydrate, **4 g** fiber, **27 g** protein

Lasagna

Prep: 35 minutes   Bake: 30 minutes   Stand: 10 minutes

¾	pound ground beef, ground pork, bulk pork sausage, or bulk Italian sausage	¼	teaspoon pepper
1	cup chopped onion (1 large)	6	dried lasagna noodles
2	cloves garlic, minced	1	beaten egg
1	7½-ounce can tomatoes, cut up	1	15-ounce container ricotta cheese or 2 cups cream-style cottage cheese, drained
1	8-ounce can tomato sauce	¼	cup grated Parmesan or Romano cheese
1	6-ounce can tomato paste	3	tablespoons snipped fresh parsley (optional)
2	teaspoons dried basil, crushed	6	ounces sliced or shredded mozzarella cheese
1	teaspoon dried oregano, crushed		Grated Parmesan cheese (optional)
1	teaspoon fennel seed, crushed (optional)		

For meat sauce, in a medium saucepan cook meat, onion, and garlic until meat is browned. Drain off fat.

Stir in undrained tomatoes, tomato sauce, tomato paste, basil, oregano, fennel seed (if desired), and pepper. Bring to boiling; reduce heat. Cover and simmer 15 minutes, stirring occasionally.

Meanwhile, cook noodles according to package directions for 10 to 12 minutes or until tender but still firm. Drain noodles; rinse with cold water. Drain well.

For filling, combine the egg, ricotta or cottage cheese, the ¼ cup Parmesan or Romano cheese, and, if desired, the parsley.

Layer half of the cooked noodles in a 2-quart rectangular baking dish. Spread with half of the filling. Top with half of the meat sauce and half of the mozzarella cheese. Repeat layers. If desired, sprinkle additional Parmesan cheese on top.

Bake in a 375° oven for 30 to 35 minutes or until heated through. Let stand 10 minutes before serving. Makes 8 servings.

Make-ahead directions: Prepare as above, except after assembling, cover and refrigerate for up to 24 hours. Bake, covered, in a 375° oven for 40 minutes. Uncover; bake about 20 minutes more or until heated through. Let stand for 10 minutes before serving.

Nutrition facts per serving: 356 calories, **16 g** total fat (**8 g** saturated fat), **87 mg** cholesterol, **495 mg** sodium, **28 g** carbohydrate, **2 g** fiber, **27 g** protein

Casseroles were the rage in the 1950s, and this stick-to-the-ribs Italian classic fit the bill. The version that appeared in our 1953 cookbook fed 12 people and boasted a pound of mozzarella cheese!

The combination of lamb and eggplant is outstanding in almost any dish. But when you add to that a kaleidoscope of wonderful flavors and seasonings, including onion, garlic, oregano, red wine, cinnamon, and Parmesan cheese, it's easy to see why Moussaka has been a classic of Greek cuisine for a long, long time.

1981 Moussaka

Prep: 40 minutes   Bake: 35 minutes   Stand: 10 minutes

2 **1-pound eggplants, peeled and cut into ½-inch-thick slices**	¼ **teaspoon dried oregano, crushed**
¼ **cup cooking oil**	¼ **teaspoon ground cinnamon**
2 **pounds ground lamb or ground beef**	1 **beaten egg**
1 **cup chopped onion (1 large)**	¼ **cup margarine or butter**
1 **clove garlic, minced**	¼ **cup all-purpose flour**
1 **8-ounce can tomato sauce**	½ **teaspoon salt**
¾ **cup dry red wine**	**Dash pepper**
2 **tablespoons snipped fresh parsley**	2 **cups milk**
¾ **teaspoon salt**	3 **eggs**
	½ **cup grated Parmesan cheese**
	Ground cinnamon
	Snipped fresh parsley (optional)

Brush both sides of eggplant slices with the oil. In a large skillet brown eggplant slices over medium heat about 2 minutes per side. Drain; set aside.

In the same skillet cook ground lamb or beef, half at a time, until meat is browned, cooking the onion and garlic with the second batch of meat. Drain off fat. Return all of meat to skillet. Stir in the tomato sauce, wine, the 2 tablespoons parsley, the ¾ teaspoon salt, oregano, and the ¼ teaspoon cinnamon. Bring to boiling; reduce heat. Simmer, uncovered, for 10 minutes or until most of the liquid is absorbed. Cool mixture slightly. Stir ½ cup of the meat mixture into the 1 beaten egg. Stir egg mixture into meat mixture in skillet.

Meanwhile, in a medium saucepan melt the margarine or butter. Stir in the flour, the ½ teaspoon salt, and pepper. Add milk all at once. Cook and stir until thickened and bubbly. Cook and stir for 1 minute more. In a medium bowl beat the 3 eggs. Gradually stir the thickened milk mixture into eggs.

In a 3-quart rectangular baking dish arrange half of the eggplant slices. Spread the meat mixture over the eggplant slices; top with remaining eggplant slices. Pour the hot egg mixture over all. Top with Parmesan cheese and sprinkle lightly with additional cinnamon.

Bake in a 325° oven for 35 to 40 minutes or until edges are bubbly. Let stand 10 minutes before serving. Cut into squares to serve. If desired, sprinkle with additional parsley. Makes 8 to 10 servings.

Nutrition facts per serving: 468 calories, **30 g** total fat (**13 g** saturated fat), **207 mg** cholesterol, **822 mg** sodium, **17 g** carbohydrate, **4 g** fiber, **29 g** protein

 **Taco Salad**

Prep: 30 minutes   Bake: 15 minutes

1	recipe Tortilla Cups* (see below)
½	pound lean ground beef or ground raw turkey
3	cloves garlic, minced
1	15-ounce can dark red kidney beans, rinsed and drained
1	8-ounce jar taco sauce
¾	cup frozen whole kernel corn (optional)
1	tablespoon chili powder
6	cups shredded leaf or iceberg lettuce
2	medium tomatoes, chopped
1	large green sweet pepper, chopped
½	cup thinly sliced green onions (4)
1	medium avocado, pitted, peeled, and sliced (optional)
¾	cup shredded sharp cheddar cheese (3 ounces)
	Dairy sour cream (optional)
	Taco sauce or salsa (optional)

Prepare Tortilla Cups; set aside. In a medium skillet cook ground beef or turkey and garlic until juices run clear. Drain off fat. Stir in kidney beans, taco sauce, corn (if desired), and chili powder. Bring to boiling; reduce heat. Cover and simmer for 10 minutes.

Meanwhile, combine lettuce, tomatoes, sweet pepper, and green onions. To serve, divide lettuce mixture among the Tortilla Cups. Top each serving with some of the meat mixture and, if desired, avocado. Sprinkle with cheese. If desired, serve with sour cream and additional taco sauce or salsa. Serves 6.

Tortilla Cups: Lightly brush six 9- or 10-inch flour tortillas with a small amount of water or spray nonstick cooking spray onto 1 side of each tortilla. Coat 6 small oven-safe bowls or six 16-ounce individual casseroles with nonstick cooking spray. Press tortillas, coated sides up, into bowls or casseroles. Place a ball of foil in each tortilla cup. Bake in a 350° oven for 15 to 20 minutes or until light brown. Remove the foil; cool. Remove Tortilla Cups from the bowls. Serve cups immediately or store in an airtight container for up to 5 days.

Note: If desired, omit Tortilla Cups and serve on individual salad plates.

Nutrition facts per serving: 366 calories, **14 g** total fat (**5 g** saturated fat), **39 mg** cholesterol, **738 mg** sodium, **47 g** carbohydrate, **6 g** fiber, **21 g** protein

Inventive cooks during the 1960s developed this hearty salad as a spin-off of the ever-popular hand-held taco.

Americans traveling abroad in the 1970s brought this classic stew from bistro menus in France to kitchen tables at home. It stars cubes of beef chuck roast seasoned with an aromatic blend of garlic, Burgundy, thyme, and marjoram.

Beef Bourguignonne
Prep: 40 minutes   Cook: 1¼ hours

1 pound boneless beef chuck roast, cut into ¾-inch cubes	3 cups whole fresh mushrooms
2 tablespoons cooking oil	4 medium carrots, cut into ¾-inch-long pieces
1 cup chopped onion (1 large)	8 ounces pearl onions or 2 cups frozen small whole onions
1 clove garlic, minced	
1½ cups Burgundy	¼ cup cold water
¾ cup beef broth	2 tablespoons all-purpose flour
1 teaspoon dried thyme, crushed	
¾ teaspoon dried marjoram, crushed	2 slices bacon, crisp-cooked, drained, and crumbled
½ teaspoon salt	
¼ teaspoon pepper	
2 bay leaves	3 cups hot cooked noodles

In a large pot or Dutch oven cook half of the meat in 1 tablespoon of the hot oil until meat is browned; remove meat from pan. Add remaining oil, remaining meat, the chopped onion, and garlic. Cook until meat is browned and onion is tender. Drain off fat. Return all meat to pot or Dutch oven.

   Stir in Burgundy, beef broth, thyme, marjoram, salt, pepper, and bay leaves. Bring to boiling; reduce heat. Cover and simmer 45 minutes. Add mushrooms, carrots, and the pearl onions. Return to boiling; reduce heat. Cover and cook for about 30 minutes more or until tender. Discard bay leaves.

Combine cold water and flour; stir into meat mixture. Cook and stir until thickened and bubbly. Cook and stir 1 minute more. Stir in bacon. Serve with noodles. Makes 6 servings.

Crockery-cooker directions: Brown meat, chopped onion, and garlic in hot oil as on opposite page. In a 3½- or 4-quart electric crockery cooker layer mushrooms, carrots, and pearl onions. Sprinkle with 3 tablespoons quick-cooking tapioca. Place meat mixture atop vegetables. Add thyme, marjoram, salt, pepper, and bay leaves. Pour only 1¼ cups burgundy and ½ cup beef broth over meat. Cover; cook on low-heat setting 10 to 12 hours or on high-heat setting 5 to 6 hours or until vegetables are tender. Discard bay leaves. Stir in bacon. Serve with noodles.

Nutrition facts per serving: 405 calories, **13 g** total fat (**3 g** saturated fat), **83 mg** cholesterol, **434 mg** sodium, **38 g** carbohydrate, **5 g** fiber, **26 g** protein

Irish-Italian Spaghetti
Prep: 15 minutes   Cook: 20 minutes

1 **pound ground beef**	¼ **teaspoon ground black pepper**
½ **cup chopped onion**	
1 **10¾-ounce can condensed cream of mushroom soup**	¼ to ½ **teaspoon bottled hot pepper sauce**
	Dash ground red pepper
1 **10¾-ounce can condensed tomato soup**	10 to 12 **ounces dried spaghetti**
½ **teaspoon dried Italian seasoning, crushed**	**Shredded Parmesan cheese (optional)**
½ **teaspoon chili powder**	

In a large saucepan or a Dutch oven cook the ground beef and onion until meat is browned and onion is tender. Drain off fat. Stir in the mushroom soup, tomato soup, Italian seasoning, chili powder, black pepper, hot pepper sauce, and red pepper. Bring to boiling; reduce heat. Cover and simmer 20 minutes.

Meanwhile, cook spaghetti according to package directions; drain well. Serve sauce over hot spaghetti. If desired, serve with Parmesan cheese. Makes 6 servings.

Nutrition facts per serving: 425 calories, **15 g** total fat (**5 g** saturated fat), **48 mg** cholesterol, **808 mg** sodium, **50 g** carbohydrate, **2 g** fiber, **23 g** protein

Irish-Italian Spaghetti is a fun recipe that uses canned soup as a speedy way to create a sauce that's both creamy and tomatoey. Add some ground beef, onion, and spicy seasonings and you have a weeknight winner that deserves a place in your repertoire of trusted favorites.

A family favorite as long as anyone can remember, Beef Pot Roast requires long, slow simmering. Our 1937 recipe cooked for 2½ to 3 hours on the range top. With this mouthwatering, up-to-date version, you can make it the traditional way, slide it in the oven and move on to other tasks, or let it simmer in your crockery cooker while you're away.

 Beef Pot Roast

Prep: 15 minutes   Cook: 1¾ hours

1 2½- to 3-pound boneless beef chuck pot roast	12 ounces whole tiny new potatoes or
2 tablespoons cooking oil	2 medium potatoes
¾ cup water, dry wine, or tomato juice	or sweet potatoes
1 tablespoon Worcestershire sauce	8 small carrots or parsnips
1 teaspoon instant beef bouillon granules	2 small onions, cut into wedges
1 teaspoon dried basil, crushed	2 stalks celery, bias-sliced into 1-inch pieces
	½ cup cold water
	¼ cup all-purpose flour

Trim fat from roast. In a 4- to 6-quart pot or Dutch oven brown roast on all sides in hot oil. Drain off fat. Combine the ¾ cup water, wine, or tomato juice; the Worcestershire sauce; bouillon granules; and basil. Pour over roast. Bring to boiling; reduce heat. Cover and simmer for 1 hour.

Meanwhile, if using new potatoes, peel a strip of skin from the center of each. If using medium potatoes or sweet potatoes, peel and quarter. Add potatoes, carrots or parsnips, onions, and celery to meat. Return to boiling; reduce heat. Cover and simmer for 45 to 60 minutes more or until tender, adding water if necessary. Transfer meat and vegetables to a platter, reserving juices in pot or Dutch oven. Keep warm.

For gravy, measure juices; skim off fat. If necessary, add enough water to juices to make 1½ cups liquid. Return to pot. Stir together the ½ cup cold water and flour. Stir into juices. Cook and stir over medium heat until thickened and bubbly. Cook and stir for 1 minute more. If desired, season with salt and pepper. Serve with meat and vegetables. Serves 8 to 10.

Oven directions: Trim fat from roast. Brown roast as directed. Combine the ¾ cup water, Worcestershire sauce, bouillon granules, and basil. Pour over roast. Bake, covered, in a 325° oven for 1 hour. Prepare potatoes as directed. Add vegetables to meat. Bake for 45 to 60 minutes more or until tender. Continue as directed.

Crockery-cooker directions: Trim fat from roast. Brown roast as directed. Thinly slice vegetables; place in a 3½- or 4-quart electric crockery cooker. Cut roast to fit; place atop vegetables. Combine the ¾ cup water, Worcestershire sauce, bouillon granules, and basil. Add to cooker. Cover and cook on low-heat setting for 10 to 12 hours. Continue as directed.

Nutrition facts per serving: 356 calories, **12 g** total fat (**4 g** saturated fat), **103 mg** cholesterol, **255 mg** sodium, **24 g** carbohydrate, **3 g** fiber, **36 g** protein

1953 Sweet-and-Sour Pork

Start to finish: 50 minutes

1	pound lean boneless pork	⅛	teaspoon ground red or black pepper
1	8-ounce can pineapple chunks (juice pack)		Shortening or cooking oil for deep frying
⅓	cup sugar	1	tablespoon cooking oil
¼	cup vinegar	1	cup bias-sliced carrots (2 medium)
2	tablespoons cornstarch		
2	tablespoons soy sauce	2	cloves garlic, minced
1	teaspoon instant chicken bouillon granules	1	large green or red sweet pepper, cut into ½-inch pieces
1	beaten egg		
¼	cup cornstarch	2	cups hot cooked rice
¼	cup all-purpose flour		
¼	cup cold water		

Trim fat from meat. Cut meat into ¾-inch cubes. For sauce, drain pineapple, reserving juice. Add enough water to juice to equal 1½ cups liquid. Stir in sugar, vinegar, the 2 tablespoons cornstarch, soy sauce, and bouillon granules. Set aside.

For batter, in a bowl combine egg, the ¼ cup cornstarch, flour, cold water, and ground red or black pepper. Stir until smooth. Dip pork into batter. Fry pork, one-third at a time, in hot oil (365°) for 4 to 5 minutes or until pork is no longer pink and batter is golden. Drain on paper towels.

Pour the 1 tablespoon oil into a wok or large skillet. (Add more oil as necessary during cooking.) Preheat over medium-high heat. Stir-fry carrots and garlic in hot oil for 1 minute. Add sweet pepper; stir-fry for 1 to 2 minutes or until crisp-tender. Push from center of wok.

Stir sauce. Pour into center of wok. Cook and stir until thickened and bubbly. Cook and stir 1 minute more. Stir in pork and pineapple. Heat through. Serve over rice. Makes 5 servings.

Nutrition facts per serving: 500 calories, **20 g** total fat (**5 g** saturated fat), **83 mg** cholesterol, **652 mg** sodium, **62 g** carbohydrate, **2 g** fiber, **18 g** protein

Our 1953 version of this Oriental standard was labeled an "economy" recipe because it stretched 1½ pounds of meat to feed six people. With today's trend toward lighter meals, the current recipe, which serves five, calls for just a pound of pork.

This 1937 recipe lets you know right away that long-ago cooks knew a thing or two about barbecued ribs. The first clue is a deep-red barbecue sauce that sends a message from your eyes to your tastebuds that it's time for action! And you'll notice plenty of sauce stickin' to those ribs because this is a sauce that simply couldn't cling more perfectly.

1937 Barbecued Ribs

Prep: 25 minutes   Bake: 1½ hours

3 to 4 pounds pork loin back ribs	1 teaspoon paprika
¾ cup catsup	1 teaspoon chili powder
¾ cup water	¼ to ½ teaspoon ground
2 tablespoons vinegar	red pepper
2 tablespoons Worcestershire sauce	2 medium onions, finely chopped (1 cup)

If desired, cut ribs into serving-size pieces. In a large shallow roasting pan place the ribs, bone sides down. Bake, covered, in a 350° oven for 1 hour. Carefully drain off liquid in roasting pan.

Meanwhile, combine catsup, water, vinegar, Worcestershire sauce, paprika, chili powder, red pepper, ½ teaspoon ground black pepper, and ¼ teaspoon salt. Stir in onions. Pour over ribs. Bake, uncovered, for 30 minutes more or until ribs are tender, basting once with sauce. Pass sauce with ribs. Serves 6.

Nutrition facts per serving: 270 calories, **17 g** total fat (**7 g** saturated fat), **67 mg** cholesterol, **600 mg** sodium, **13 g** carbohydrate, **1 g** fiber, **17 g** protein

The Baked Ham in the 1930 edition of our cookbook was scored and studded with cloves just as this one is. However instead of orange juice, the brown sugar glaze used "enough vinegar to smooth to a thick sauce."

1930 Glazed Ham

Prep: 15 minutes   Bake: 1½ hours   Stand: 15 minutes

1 5- to 6-pound cooked ham (rump half or shank portion)	1 cup orange juice
	½ cup packed brown sugar
24 whole cloves	4 teaspoons cornstarch
2 teaspoons finely shredded orange peel	1½ teaspoons dry mustard

Score ham by making diagonal cuts in a diamond pattern. To stud with cloves, push long clove ends into scored intersections in ham. Place ham on rack in shallow roasting pan. Insert a meat thermometer. Bake in a 325° oven until thermometer registers 125°. For rump, bake 1¼ to 1½ hours; for shank, bake 1¾ to 2 hours.

For glaze, in saucepan combine remaining ingredients. Cook and stir over medium heat until thickened and bubbly. Cook and stir 2 minutes more. Brush over ham. Bake 15 to 30 minutes more or until thermometer registers 135°. Let stand 15 minutes before carving. (The meat's temperature will rise 5° during standing.) Pass remaining glaze. Makes 16 to 20 servings.

Nutrition facts per serving: 351 calories, **22 g** total fat (**7 g** saturated fat), **88 mg** cholesterol, **1,335 mg** sodium, **8 g** carbohydrate, **0 g** fiber, **29 g** protein

1930 Roasted Chicken
Prep: 10 minutes   Roast: 1¼ hours

1	3½- to 4-pound whole chicken
	Salt (optional)
1	small onion, quartered (optional)
2	stalks celery, cut up (optional)
	Cooking oil
	Dried thyme or oregano, crushed (optional)

Rinse chicken; pat dry with paper towels. If desired, rub inside of body cavity with salt. If desired, place onions and celery in body cavity. Skewer neck skin to back; tie legs to tail. Twist wing tips under back. Place chicken, breast side up, on a rack in a shallow roasting pan; brush with cooking oil and, if desired, sprinkle with herb.

If desired, insert a meat thermometer into center of an inside thigh muscle. Do not allow thermometer bulb to touch bone. Roast, uncovered, in a 375° oven for 1¼ to 1¾ hours or until drumsticks move easily in their sockets, chicken is no longer pink, and meat thermometer registers 180° to 185°. Remove chicken from oven; cover and let stand 10 minutes before carving. Makes 6 to 8 servings.

Nutrition facts per serving: 264 calories, **16 g** total fat (**4 g** saturated fat), **92 mg** cholesterol, **85 mg** sodium, **0 g** carbohydrate, **0 g** fiber, **29 g** protein

Not all 1930s' cooks had the luxury of starting with a ready-to-cook chicken for roasting. For those who had to clean their own birds, our cookbook listed complete directions for removing the internal organs and singeing the pin feathers. Times sure have changed!

For an attractive presentation, garnish the serving platter with kumquats, fresh bay leaves, and fresh herbs.

Chicken Parmesan

Prep: 20 minutes   Bake: 45 minutes

1 **cup packaged herb stuffing mix, crushed**	2½ **to 3 pounds meaty chicken pieces (breasts, thighs, and/or drumsticks)**
⅔ **cup grated Parmesan cheese**	
¼ **cup snipped fresh parsley**	¼ **cup margarine or butter, melted**
¼ **teaspoon garlic powder**	

In a shallow dish combine the stuffing mix, Parmesan cheese, parsley, and garlic powder; set aside. Skin the chicken. Rinse chicken; pat dry. Brush chicken with margarine; coat with stuffing mixture.

In a greased 15×10×1-inch or 13×9×2-inch baking pan, arrange chicken so the pieces do not touch. Bake, uncovered, in a 375° oven for 45 to 55 minutes or until tender and no longer pink. Do not turn pieces while baking. Makes 6 servings.

Nutrition facts per serving: 335 calories, **18 g** total fat (**5 g** saturated fat), **85 mg** cholesterol, **558 mg** sodium, **12 g** carbohydrate, **0 g** fiber, **31 g** protein

Country Captain

Prep: 20 minutes   Cook: 35 minutes

2 **to 2½ pounds meaty chicken pieces (breasts, thighs, and/or drumsticks)**	1 **teaspoon instant chicken bouillon granules**
	½ **teaspoon ground mace or nutmeg**
1 **14½-ounce can stewed tomatoes**	¼ **teaspoon sugar**
¼ **cup currants or raisins**	1 **tablespoon cornstarch**
2 **to 3 teaspoons curry powder**	3 **cups hot cooked rice**
	2 **tablespoons snipped fresh Italian parsley**

Skin chicken. Rinse chicken; pat dry. In a large skillet stir together undrained tomatoes, currants or raisins, curry powder, bouillon granules, mace or nutmeg, and sugar. Place chicken in skillet. Spoon sauce over chicken. Bring mixture to boiling; reduce heat. Cover and simmer 35 to 45 minutes or until chicken is tender and no longer pink. Remove chicken from skillet; keep warm.

For sauce, skim fat from mixture in skillet. In a small bowl stir together cornstarch and 1 tablespoon cold water; add to skillet. Cook and stir until thickened and bubbly. Cook and stir for 2 minutes more. Serve sauce over hot rice and chicken. Sprinkle with parsley. Makes 6 servings.

Nutrition facts per serving: 277 calories, **5 g** total fat (**1 g** saturated fat), **61 mg** cholesterol, **380 mg** sodium, **33 g** carbohydrate, **2 g** fiber, **23 g** protein

Barbecued Chicken
Prep: 25 minutes   Bake: 50 minutes

2 to 2½ pounds meaty chicken pieces (breasts, thighs, and/or drumsticks)	1 cup catsup
2 tablespoons cooking oil	2 tablespoons brown sugar
2 medium onions, cut into ¼-inch-thick slices	2 tablespoons lemon juice
½ cup chopped celery	2 tablespoons Worcestershire sauce
	2 tablespoons prepared mustard

Skin chicken. Rinse chicken; pat dry. In a large skillet heat oil. Add chicken to skillet. Cook, uncovered, over medium heat for 10 minutes, turning occasionally to brown evenly. Transfer chicken to a 2-quart rectangular baking dish; set aside.

Add the onions and celery to skillet; cook about 5 minutes or until tender. Meanwhile, in a medium bowl combine catsup, brown sugar, lemon juice, Worcestershire sauce, and mustard. Add to skillet; bring to boiling. Remove from heat; spoon over chicken in baking dish.

Bake chicken, covered, in a 375° oven for 40 minutes. Uncover; baste with sauce. Bake, uncovered, for 10 to 15 minutes more or until chicken is tender and no longer pink, basting once or twice with sauce. Transfer chicken to serving platter. Skim fat from sauce; pass sauce with chicken. Makes 6 servings.

Nutrition facts per serving: 234 calories, **9 g** total fat (**2 g** saturated fat), **54 mg** cholesterol, **714 mg** sodium, **20 g** carbohydrate, **1 g** fiber, **18 g** protein

Here's a simple supper dish that the whole family will love. The secret is in how the delicious sauce is made. It's stirred together in the same skillet the chicken is browned in, incorporating those zesty little bits of flavor that are always left clinging to the pan. This lets you build a rich and tangy sauce you won't forget.

Maryland Fried Chicken
Start to finish: 1 hour

1 **beaten egg**	2½ **to 3 pounds meaty**
3 **tablespoons milk**	**chicken pieces**
1 **cup finely crushed**	**(breasts, thighs,**
saltine crackers	**and/or drumsticks)**
(about 28)	2 **tablespoons cooking oil**
1 **teaspoon dried thyme,**	1 **cup milk**
crushed	1 **recipe Cream Gravy**
½ **teaspoon paprika**	**(see below) (optional)**
⅛ **teaspoon pepper**	**Hot mashed potatoes**
	(optional)

In a small bowl combine the egg and the 3 tablespoons milk. In a shallow bowl combine the crackers, thyme, paprika, and pepper. Set aside.

Skin chicken. Rinse chicken and pat dry with paper towels. Dip chicken pieces, 1 at a time, in the egg mixture. Roll in cracker mixture.

In a large skillet heat oil. Add chicken to skillet. Cook, uncovered, over medium heat for 10 minutes, turning occasionally to brown evenly. Drain off fat. Add the 1 cup milk to skillet. Reduce heat to medium-low; cover tightly. Cook chicken for 35 minutes. Uncover; cook for 5 to 10 minutes more or until chicken is tender and no longer pink. If desired, prepare Cream Gravy and serve with mashed potatoes. Makes 6 servings.

Cream Gravy: Transfer chicken to a serving platter; keep warm. Skim fat from drippings in skillet. In a screw-top jar combine ¾ cup milk, 3 tablespoons all-purpose flour, ¼ teaspoon salt, and ⅛ teaspoon pepper; shake until well mixed. Add to the skillet. Stir in 1 cup milk. Cook and stir over medium heat until thickened and bubbly. Cook and stir for 1 minute more. If necessary, thin with additional milk. Makes 1½ cups gravy.

Nutrition facts per serving: 327 calories, **13 g** total fat (**4 g** saturated fat), **121 mg** cholesterol, **410 mg** sodium, **19 g** carbohydrate, **0 g** fiber, **31 g** protein

Chicken Cassoulet

Prep: 1 hour 20 minutes   Cook: 4½ to 11 hours

1 **cup dry navy beans (7 to 8 ounces)**	1 **teaspoon instant beef or chicken bouillon granules**
2½ **to 3 pounds meaty chicken pieces (breasts, thighs, and/or drumsticks)**	½ **teaspoon dried basil, crushed**
½ **pound cooked Polish sausage**	½ **teaspoon dried oregano, crushed**
1 **cup tomato juice**	½ **teaspoon paprika**
1 **tablespoon Worcestershire sauce**	½ **cup chopped carrot**
	½ **cup chopped celery**
	½ **cup chopped onion (1 medium)**

Rinse beans; place in a medium saucepan. Add enough water to cover beans by 2 inches. Bring to boiling; reduce heat. Simmer, uncovered, for 10 minutes. Remove from heat. Cover; let stand for 1 hour. (Or, place the beans in a large bowl. Cover with water to about 2 inches above beans. Allow to soak in a cool place overnight.) Drain and rinse beans.

Meanwhile, skin the chicken. Rinse chicken; pat dry and set aside. Halve sausage lengthwise and cut into 1-inch-thick pieces. In a medium mixing bowl combine drained beans, sausage, tomato juice, Worcestershire sauce, bouillon granules, basil, oregano, and paprika. Set aside.

In a 3½- or 4-quart electric crockery cooker combine the carrot, celery, and onion. Place chicken pieces on top. Pour bean mixture over chicken. Cover; cook on low-heat setting for 9 to 11 hours or on high-heat setting for 4½ to 5½ hours. Remove chicken and sausage with a slotted spoon. Mash bean mixture slightly. Serve chicken, sausage, and beans in soup bowls. Makes 6 servings.

Nutrition facts per serving: 381 calories, **16 g** total fat (**5 g** saturated fat), **88 mg** cholesterol, **720 mg** sodium, **26 g** carbohydrate, **4 g** fiber, **32 g** protein

There are many cassoulet versions. Some of the more classic recipes require a couple days' worth of preparation and lots of laborious steps along the way. Not this one. We've found that the bottom line for any good cassoulet is that it be hearty and satisfying. That's exactly why this is such a special cassoulet recipe: It has every bit of the goodness and none of the tedium.

One of the original comfort foods now staging a comeback, Chicken Potpie appeared in our 1937 edition. Instead of having a full pastry crust, as the current recipe does, it only sported pastry triangles on top.

 Chicken Potpies
Prep: 50 minutes
Bake: 12 minutes

Pastry for Double-Crust Pie (see page 79)
1   10-ounce package frozen peas and carrots
½   cup chopped onion (1 medium)
½   cup chopped fresh mushrooms
¼   cup margarine or butter
⅓   cup all-purpose flour
½   teaspoon salt
½   teaspoon dried sage, marjoram, or thyme, crushed

⅛   teaspoon pepper
2   cups chicken broth
¾   cup milk
3   cups cubed cooked chicken or turkey (1 pound)
¼   cup snipped fresh parsley
¼   cup diced pimiento

Prepare dough for Pastry for Double-Crust Pie; set aside. Cook peas and carrots according to package directions; drain and set aside.

In a saucepan cook onion and mushrooms in margarine or butter until tender. Stir in flour; salt; sage, marjoram, or thyme; and pepper. Add chicken broth and milk all at once. Cook and stir until thickened and bubbly. Stir in drained peas and carrots, chicken or turkey, parsley, and pimiento; cook until bubbly.

Pour mixture into six 10-ounce casseroles. (Or, use a 2-quart rectangular baking dish.)

Roll pastry into a 15×10-inch rectangle. Cut into six 5-inch circles and place atop the hot chicken mixture in the 10-ounce casseroles. (Or, roll pastry into a 13×9-inch rectangle. Place over the rectangular baking dish.) Flute edges of pastry and cut slits or tiny decorative shapes in the pastry tops for steam to escape. Bake in a 450° oven for 12 to 15 minutes or until pastry is golden brown. Serves 6.

Biscuit-Topped Chicken Potpies: Prepare as above, except omit pastry. Cut 1 package (6) refrigerated biscuits into quarters and arrange atop bubbly chicken mixture in individual casseroles or the baking dish. Bake in a 400° oven about 15 minutes or until biscuits are golden.

Nutrition facts per serving: 638 calories, **38 g** total fat (**9 g** saturated fat), **70 mg** cholesterol, **820 mg** sodium, **43 g** carbohydrate, **3 g** fiber, **31 g** protein
   Nutrition facts per Biscuit-Topped Chicken Potpie: 390 calories, **19 g** total fat (**5 g** saturated fat)

India Chicken Curry
Start to finish: 20 minutes

½ **cup finely chopped onion (1 medium)**	1 **teaspoon curry powder**
½ **cup finely chopped celery**	1½ **cups chicken broth**
2 **tablespoons margarine or butter**	½ **teaspoon Worcestershire sauce**
3 **tablespoons all-purpose flour**	1½ **cups chopped cooked chicken (8 ounces)**
	½ **cup tomato juice**
	2 **cups hot cooked rice**

In a medium saucepan cook the onion and celery in hot margarine or butter until tender. Stir in the flour and curry powder. Add the chicken broth and Worcestershire sauce. Cook and stir until thickened and bubbly. Stir in the cooked chicken and tomato juice; heat through. If desired, season to taste with salt and pepper. Serve over hot rice. Makes 4 servings.

Nutrition facts per serving: 312 calories, **11 g** total fat (**2 g** saturated fat), **51 mg** cholesterol, **539 mg** sodium, **31 g** carbohydrate, **1 g** fiber, **22 g** protein

When you see the word "curry" in a recipe title, it's hard to know what to expect because there's a wide range of spiciness. On a scale from mild to "pass the fire extinguisher," this curry rates as fairly mild, making it a great family dish. But curry fanatics shouldn't pass it by because plenty of curry flavor shines through without masking the well-balanced flavors of all the other ingredients.

Chicken à la King
Start to finish: 25 minutes

1 **cup sliced fresh mushrooms**	2½ **cups half-and-half or light cream**
¼ **cup chopped green sweet pepper**	3 **beaten egg yolks**
¼ **cup chopped onion**	2 **tablespoons dry sherry**
3 **tablespoons margarine or butter**	1 **tablespoon lemon juice**
2 **tablespoons all-purpose flour**	2 **cups cubed cooked chicken (10 ounces)**
½ **teaspoon paprika**	2 **tablespoons diced pimiento**
	24 **toast points**

In a large saucepan cook mushrooms, sweet pepper, and onion in margarine or butter until tender. Stir in flour, paprika, and ½ teaspoon salt. Add half-and-half or light cream all at once. Cook and stir until thickened and bubbly.

Stir about 1 cup of the thickened sauce into the beaten egg yolks; return to saucepan. Cook and stir over medium heat until bubbly. Stir in sherry and lemon juice. Add chicken and pimiento; heat through. Serve over toast points. Serves 6.

Nutrition facts per serving: 424 calories, **26 g** total fat (**11 g** saturated fat), **200 mg** cholesterol, **474 mg** sodium, **21 g** carbohydrate, **1 g** fiber, **25 g** protein

This homey family dish is as comforting today as it was in 1930. The creamy chicken was originally served on a bed of fried noodles. The updated version features a sherry-flavored cream sauce and is served over more traditional toast points.

Grilled Blackened Redfish
Prep: 15 minutes   Grill: 4 minutes

4 4-ounce fresh or frozen redfish or red snapper fillets	½ teaspoon ground red pepper
½ teaspoon onion powder	½ teaspoon dried thyme, crushed
½ teaspoon ground white pepper	½ teaspoon garlic powder
½ teaspoon ground black pepper	¼ teaspoon salt
	3 tablespoons margarine or butter, melted

Thaw fish, if frozen. Measure thickness of fish. Combine the onion powder, white pepper, black pepper, red pepper, thyme, garlic powder, and salt. Brush fish with some of the melted margarine. Coat fish evenly on both sides with pepper mixture.

Remove grill rack from grill. Place a 12-inch cast-iron skillet directly on hot coals. Heat 5 minutes or until a drop of water sizzles in the skillet. Add fish to skillet. Drizzle fish with remaining melted margarine. Cook, uncovered, for 2 to 3 minutes per side for ½- to ¾-inch-thick fillets (3 to 4 minutes per side for 1-inch-thick fillets) or until fish flakes easily when tested with a fork. Makes 4 servings.

Nutrition facts per serving: 194 calories, **10 g** total fat (**2 g** saturated fat), **42 mg** cholesterol, **151 mg** sodium, **1 g** carbohydrate, **0 g** fiber, **24 g** protein

 ## Crispy Oven-Fried Fish
Prep: 15 minutes   Bake: 6 minutes

1 pound fresh or frozen skinless cod, orange roughy, or catfish fillets, about ½ inch thick	⅓ cup fine dry bread crumbs
¼ cup milk	¼ cup grated Parmesan cheese
¼ cup all-purpose flour	½ teaspoon dried dillweed
	2 tablespoons margarine or butter, melted

Thaw fish, if frozen. Grease baking sheet; set aside. Rinse fish; pat dry. Cut into 4 serving-size pieces. Place milk in shallow dish. Place flour in another shallow dish. In third shallow dish mix crumbs, cheese, dillweed, and ⅛ teaspoon pepper. Toss with melted margarine. Dip fish in milk, then in flour. Dip again in milk, then in crumb mixture to coat all sides. Place on prepared baking sheet. Bake, uncovered, in 450° oven for 6 to 9 minutes or until fish flakes easily when tested with a fork. Serves 4.

Nutrition facts per serving: 232 calories, **9 g** total fat (**3 g** saturated fat), **51 mg** cholesterol, **316 mg** sodium, **13 g** carbohydrate, **1 g** fiber, **24 g** protein

Chilled Salmon Steaks with Lemon-Dill Dressing
Prep: 15 minutes
Cook: 8 minutes
Chill: 2 hours

  6 fresh or frozen salmon
     or halibut steaks,
     1 to 1¼ inches thick
     (about 2 pounds total)
1½ cups water
  ¼ cup lemon juice
  1 medium onion, sliced
 10 whole black peppercorns
  3 sprigs fresh parsley
  2 bay leaves
  ½ teaspoon salt
  1 recipe Lemon-Dill
     Dressing (see below)
     Fresh dill sprigs

Thaw fish, if frozen. Rinse fish and pat dry with paper towels; set aside. In a 12-inch skillet combine water, lemon juice, onion, peppercorns, parsley, bay leaves, and salt. Bring to boiling; add fish steaks. Return to boiling; reduce heat. Cover; simmer for 8 to 12 minutes or until fish flakes easily when tested with a fork. Remove fish from skillet; discard poaching liquid. Cover; chill in refrigerator about 2 hours or until chilled thoroughly. Serve with Lemon-Dill Dressing. If desired, garnish with fresh dill sprigs. Makes 6 servings.

Lemon-Dill Dressing: In a small mixing bowl stir together ¾ cup mayonnaise or salad dressing, 3 tablespoons buttermilk, 2 tablespoons snipped fresh dill or 2 teaspoons dried dillweed, 1 tablespoon snipped fresh chives, ½ teaspoon finely shredded lemon peel, and 2 teaspoons lemon juice. Cover and chill in refrigerator at least 1 hour.

Nutrition facts per serving: 339 calories, **27 g** total fat (**4 g** saturated fat), **43 mg** cholesterol, **433 mg** sodium, **1 g** carbohydrate, **0 g** fiber, **22 g** protein

Interest in fish and seafood has blossomed in recent decades. This elegant chilled salmon recipe from the most recent edition of our red plaid cookbook is an example of the type of restaurant dish Americans now want to make at home. Our creamy dressing features a mixture of fresh dill and lemon, both traditional seasonings for salmon.

Supper Corn Chowder
Start to finish: 25 minutes

3	slices bacon	1½	cups chopped cooked
1	medium onion,		potatoes
	chopped	1	10¾-ounce can
2	cups milk		condensed cream
2	cups cooked or canned		of mushroom soup
	whole kernel corn	½	teaspoon dried thyme,
			crushed (optional)

In large saucepan cook bacon until crisp. Remove bacon, reserving 1 tablespoon drippings. Drain bacon on paper towels; crumble and set aside. Cook onion in reserved drippings until tender. Stir in milk, corn, potatoes, soup, thyme (if desired), and dash pepper. Bring to boiling; reduce heat. Simmer, uncovered, for 2 minutes. If desired, mash slightly. Ladle into bowls; sprinkle bacon over each serving. Makes 4 servings.

Nutrition facts per serving: 331 calories, **12 g** total fat (**4 g** saturated fat), **14 mg** cholesterol, **772 mg** sodium, **50 g** carbohydrate, **5 g** fiber, **11 g** protein

 Macaroni-Cheese Puff
Prep: 30 minutes   Bake: 50 minutes

½	cup dried elbow	1	cup soft bread crumbs
	macaroni	¼	cup diced pimiento
1½	cups milk	1	tablespoon snipped
6	ounces sharp process		fresh parsley
	American cheese	1	tablespoon finely
	slices, torn		chopped onion
3	tablespoons margarine	3	egg whites
	or butter	¼	teaspoon cream
3	egg yolks		of tartar

Cook macaroni according to package directions. Drain; set aside. Meanwhile, in a large saucepan combine the milk, cheese, and margarine or butter. Cook and stir over low heat until cheese is melted. Remove from heat. In a small bowl beat the egg yolks. Stir about ½ cup of the hot cheese mixture into the egg yolks. Pour egg yolk mixture into saucepan, stirring to combine. Add the drained macaroni, bread crumbs, pimiento, parsley, and onion. Set aside.

Beat egg whites and cream of tartar until stiff peaks form (tips stand straight). Gently fold into macaroni mixture. Pour mixture into ungreased 1½-quart soufflé dish. Bake in a 325° oven for 50 minutes. Serve immediately. Serves 6.

Nutrition facts per serving: 284 calories, **19 g** total fat (**8 g** saturated fat), **138 mg** cholesterol, **574 mg** sodium, **15 g** carbohydrate, **1 g** fiber, **13 g** protein

Corn chowder has been a family mainstay for many years—we can't imagine it ever going out of style. Nonetheless, we've altered this recipe a bit since 1953. Originally, it was served with a pat of butter floating in each bowlful—a presentation today's more health-conscious society can easily do without.

For us, this recipe is the ultimate macaroni and cheese. Its feather-light, soufflélike consistency distinguishes it from much heavier baked versions, but the flavor is every bit as rich and creamy.

1981 Choose-a-Flavor Quiche
Prep: 25 minutes   Bake: 35 minutes   Stand: 10 minutes

Pastry for Single-Crust Pie (see page 79)	¾ cup chopped cooked ham, chicken, or crabmeat
3 beaten eggs	
1½ cups milk	1½ cups shredded Swiss, cheddar, Monterey Jack, or Havarti cheese (6 ounces)
¼ cup sliced green onions (2)	
¼ teaspoon salt	
⅛ teaspoon pepper	1 tablespoon all-purpose flour
Dash ground nutmeg	

Prepare pastry and line pie plate as directed. Line unpricked pastry shell with a double thickness of heavy-duty foil. Bake in a 450° oven for 5 minutes. Remove foil. Bake for 5 to 7 minutes more or until pastry is nearly done. Remove from oven. Reduce oven temperature to 325°.

Meanwhile, in bowl stir together eggs, milk, green onions, salt, pepper, and nutmeg. Stir in ham, chicken, or crabmeat. Toss together the cheese and flour. Add to egg mixture; mix well. Pour egg mixture into hot pastry shell. To prevent overbrowning, cover edge of crust with foil. Bake in the 325° oven for 35 to 40 minutes or until knife inserted near center comes out clean. Let stand 10 minutes before serving. Makes 6 servings.

Nutrition facts per serving: 393 calories, **24 g** total fat (**10 g** saturated fat), **146 mg** cholesterol, **525 mg** sodium, **24 g** carbohydrate, **1 g** fiber, **20 g** protein

Quiche took America by storm in the 1970s, appearing on restaurant and home menus as a popular brunch or luncheon entrée. Classic Quiche Lorraine first appeared in our 1981 edition. This delectable recipe gives you several cheese options as well as allowing you to select from ham, chicken, or crabmeat.

In days gone by, Spinach Loaf was served as a side dish. But today's trend is toward lighter meals, making it a fitting choice if you're looking for a light, yet satisfying, main dish. You'll find the zippy flavors of the accompanying tomato-bacon sauce to be a perfect foil for the refined flavor of spinach.

Spinach Loaf
Prep: 25 minutes   Bake: 20 minutes

2	10-ounce packages frozen chopped spinach, thawed	2	tablespoons chopped onion
2	beaten eggs	2	tablespoons chopped green sweet pepper
¾	cup shredded cheddar cheese (3 ounces)	2	teaspoons all-purpose flour
⅓	cup fine dry bread crumbs		Dash ground black pepper
1	tablespoon vinegar	½	cup water
½	teaspoon salt Dash ground black pepper	2	medium tomatoes, peeled, seeded, and chopped
4	slices bacon, chopped		

Squeeze excess liquid from spinach; set aside. In a mixing bowl combine the eggs, cheese, bread crumbs, vinegar, salt, and dash black pepper. Stir in the well-drained spinach. Pat mixture into a greased 8×4×2-inch loaf pan. (At this point, loaf may be covered and refrigerated overnight before baking.)

Bake, uncovered, in a 400° oven for 20 to 25 minutes or until a knife inserted in the center comes out clean.

Meanwhile, in a medium skillet cook bacon until crisp. Remove from skillet, reserving 2 teaspoons of the drippings. Drain bacon on paper towels. Cook onion and sweet pepper in hot drippings over medium heat for 5 minutes or until tender. Stir in the flour and dash black pepper. Gradually stir in water. Cook and stir until thickened and bubbly. Cook and stir 1 minute more. Stir in bacon and tomatoes; heat through. To serve, invert loaf onto platter. Cut loaf into slices; serve with sauce. Makes 8 servings.

Nutrition facts per serving: 118 calories, **7 g** total fat (**3 g** saturated fat), **67 mg** cholesterol, **340 mg** sodium, **8 g** carbohydrate, **2 g** fiber, **8 g** protein

side dishes

Scalloped Potatoes haven't changed much in 70 years. Our original recipe layered potatoes with a white sauce and a dab of butter. Today's version includes a little extra onion and garlic.

1930 Scalloped Potatoes

Prep: 25 minutes   Bake: 1 hour 10 minutes

½ cup chopped onion (1 medium)	¼ teaspoon pepper
1 clove garlic, minced	Dash salt
2 tablespoons margarine or butter	1¼ cups milk
2 tablespoons all-purpose flour	1 pound potatoes (such as long white, round white, round red, or yellow)

Grease a 1½-quart casserole; set aside. For sauce, in a small saucepan cook onion and garlic in margarine or butter until tender. Stir in flour, pepper, and salt. Add milk all at once. Cook and stir over medium heat until thickened and bubbly.

Thinly slice potatoes. Place half of the potatoes in prepared casserole. Cover with half the sauce. Repeat layers.

Bake, covered, in a 350° oven for 40 minutes. Uncover and bake about 30 minutes more or until potatoes are tender. Makes 4 to 6 servings.

Nutrition facts per serving: 228 calories, **7 g** total fat (**2 g** saturated fat), **6 mg** cholesterol, **148 mg** sodium, **35 g** carbohydrate, **1 g** fiber, **6 g** protein

Take a big, creamy mound of mashed potatoes, shape it into a volcanic cone, add a little cheese and cream, and—oh boy!—you just created an all-time kid favorite. And whether you're a kid or just a kid at heart, you'll love this deliciously playful treatment of classic mashed potatoes.

1953 Volcano Potatoes

Prep: 35 minutes   Bake: 20 minutes

1½ pounds baking potatoes (4 to 5 medium)	⅛ teaspoon pepper
1 to 3 tablespoons milk	½ cup whipping cream
½ teaspoon salt	½ cup shredded sharp or regular American cheese (2 ounces)

Peel and quarter potatoes. In covered saucepan cook potatoes in a small amount of boiling water 20 to 25 minutes or until tender; drain. Mash with potato masher or beat with electric mixer on low speed. Gradually beat in enough of the milk to make light and fluffy. Stir in salt and pepper. Grease 9-inch pie plate. Mound potatoes in pie plate, forming into a volcano shape about 3 inches tall and 5 inches across at the base. (Leave 1-inch space between potato mixture and edge of pie plate.) Make a deep hole or crater in the center of the mound.

In a small bowl whip the cream until soft peaks form; fold in cheese. Spoon cream mixture into the hole, allowing the excess to flow down side. Bake, uncovered, in a 350° oven about 20 minutes or until golden and bubbly. Serves 5.

Nutrition facts per serving: 242 calories, **13 g** total fat (**8 g** saturated fat), **44 mg** cholesterol, **393 mg** sodium, **28 g** carbohydrate, **2 g** fiber, **5 g** protein

Potatoes Floradora

Prep: 20 minutes   Bake: 35 minutes

6 potatoes (about 2 pounds), washed	1 tablespoon all-purpose flour
1 onion, finely chopped	1 teaspoon snipped fresh parsley
1 cup finely chopped fresh mushrooms	¼ teaspoon paprika
2 tablespoons margarine or butter	3 tablespoons milk
	1 beaten egg yolk

Cut a thin slice from top of each potato. Carefully scoop out potato without harming skin, leaving a ½-inch-thick shell. (If necessary, to make potatoes sit flat, cut a thin slice from bottom of each.) Place shells in a large bowl. Cover with water until needed. Finely chop scooped-out potato.

In a large skillet cook chopped potato, onion, and mushrooms in hot margarine until onion is tender. Stir in flour, parsley, paprika, ½ teaspoon salt, and ¼ teaspoon pepper. Cook until golden. Add milk; cook and stir until slightly thickened. Stir into beaten egg yolk. Drain potato shells and fill with cooked potato mixture. Place in shallow baking pan. Bake potatoes, uncovered, in a 450° oven about 35 minutes or until potato shells are tender. Makes 6 servings.

Nutrition facts per serving: 216 calories, **5 g** total fat (**1 g** saturated fat), **36 mg** cholesterol, **240 mg** sodium, **39 g** carbohydrate, **2 g** fiber, **5 g** protein

During the Depression, finding creative ways to dress up ordinary ingredients was important. Potatoes Floradora offers a terrific example of how to make a lot out of a little. Hollowed potato jackets are filled with sautéed onion, mushrooms, potato, and a few seasonings, then baked. This makes a pretty presentation, as well as a delicious dish that is eminently satisfying.

Sweet Potato-Cashew Bake

Prep: 20 minutes   Bake: 1 hour

6 medium sweet potatoes	½ teaspoon ground ginger
1 16-ounce package frozen unsweetened peach slices	2 tablespoons margarine or butter
½ cup packed brown sugar	¼ cup coarsely chopped cashews

Peel potatoes and cut into ½-inch-thick slices. In a 2-quart rectangular baking dish layer half of the potato slices and half of the peach slices. In a small bowl combine brown sugar and ginger. Sprinkle half of mixture over potatoes and peaches. Repeat layers. Dot with margarine or butter. Bake, covered, in a 350° oven for 45 minutes, stirring once. Uncover; sprinkle with cashews. Bake, uncovered, about 15 minutes more or until potatoes are tender. Spoon cooking juices over potatoes and peaches before serving. Makes 6 to 8 servings.

Nutrition facts per serving: 278 calories, **7 g** total fat (**1 g** saturated fat), **0 mg** cholesterol, **89 mg** sodium, **54 g** carbohydrate, **6 g** fiber, **4 g** protein

Sweet potatoes are usually served baked, candied, or with marshmallows (and that's just dandy!), but they do deserve a little more variety. Here's a nice departure from the routine. Peaches, cashews, and ginger complement this surprisingly versatile vegetable in a simple and homey dish.

 Asparagus-Tomato Stir-Fry
Start to finish: 25 minutes

¾ pound fresh asparagus spears or one 10-ounce package frozen cut asparagus	4 green onions, bias-sliced into 1-inch lengths (½ cup)
¼ cup chicken broth	1½ cups sliced fresh mushrooms
2 teaspoons soy sauce	2 small tomatoes, cut into thin wedges
1 teaspoon cornstarch	
1 tablespoon cooking oil	
½ teaspoon grated fresh ginger	

Snap off and discard woody bases from fresh asparagus. If desired, scrape off scales. Bias-slice asparagus into 1-inch-long pieces. (Or, thaw and drain frozen asparagus.) For sauce, combine broth, soy sauce, and cornstarch.

Pour oil into a wok or large skillet. (Add more oil as necessary during cooking.) Preheat over medium-high heat. Stir-fry ginger in hot oil 30 seconds. Add asparagus and green onions; stir-fry 3 minutes. Add mushrooms; stir-fry 1 minute more or until asparagus is crisp-tender.

Push the vegetables from center of wok. Stir sauce; add to center of wok. Cook and stir until thickened and bubbly. Add tomatoes. Stir to coat with sauce; heat through. Serves 4.

Nutrition facts per serving: 70 calories, **4 g** total fat (**1 g** saturated fat), **0 mg** cholesterol, **227 mg** sodium, **7 g** carbohydrate, **2 g** fiber, **3 g** protein

Swiss Corn Bake
Prep: 20 minutes   Bake: 25 minutes   Stand: 5 minutes

4 cups fresh corn kernels or two 10-ounce packages frozen whole kernel corn	¾ cup shredded process Swiss or Gruyère cheese (3 ounces)
2 beaten eggs	¾ cup soft bread crumbs (1 slice)
2 5-ounce cans (1⅓ cups) evaporated milk	1 tablespoon margarine or butter, melted
2 tablespoons finely chopped onion	¼ cup shredded process Swiss or Gruyère cheese (1 ounce)
¼ teaspoon salt Dash pepper	

Grease a 9-inch pie plate or an 8-inch quiche dish; set aside. In a covered medium saucepan cook fresh corn in a small amount of boiling lightly salted water for 4 minutes. (Or, cook frozen corn according to package directions.) Drain well.

In a medium mixing bowl combine drained corn, beaten eggs, milk, onion, salt, and pepper. Stir in the ¾ cup cheese. Transfer mixture to prepared pie plate or quiche dish.

In a small bowl combine soft bread crumbs and melted margarine or butter. Stir in the ¼ cup cheese. Sprinkle over corn mixture. Bake, uncovered, in a 350° oven for 25 to 35 minutes or until a knife inserted near the center comes out clean. Let stand for 5 to 10 minutes before serving. Makes 6 servings.

Nutrition facts per serving: 296 calories, **13 g** total fat (**6 g** saturated fat), **101 mg** cholesterol, **487 mg** sodium, **34 g** carbohydrate, **4 g** fiber, **14 g** protein

Isn't it a treat when something so simple to prepare turns out to be tasty as well? That's what you can expect when you make and serve Swiss Corn Bake. Cheese and corn in a creamy, custardlike setting make a perfect combination.

1945 Stuffed Zucchini Squash
Prep: 20 minutes   Bake: 20 minutes

3 medium zucchini (each 6 to 7 inches long and 5 to 6 ounces)	2 tablespoons finely chopped onion
Salt	2 tablespoons snipped fresh parsley
1 beaten egg	Dash pepper
1 tablespoon margarine or butter, melted and cooled	1½ cups soft bread crumbs (2 slices)
¼ cup grated Parmesan cheese	1 tablespoon grated Parmesan cheese

Trim ends of zucchini; do not peel. Cook whole zucchini in boiling water for 5 minutes or until crisp-tender. Cool slightly. Halve lengthwise. Scoop out pulp, leaving a ¼-inch-thick shell. Chop pulp; set aside. Sprinkle shells lightly with salt. Arrange in a 2-quart rectangular baking dish.

In a medium mixing bowl combine egg, margarine, the ¼ cup Parmesan, onion, parsley, and pepper. Stir in chopped pulp and bread crumbs; spoon filling into shells. Sprinkle with the 1 tablespoon Parmesan. Bake, uncovered, in a 350° oven about 20 minutes or until set and heated through. Serves 6.

Nutrition facts per serving: 94 calories, **5 g** total fat (**3 g** saturated fat), **45 mg** cholesterol, **210 mg** sodium, **9 g** carbohydrate, **1 g** fiber, **5 g** protein

1981 Harvest Stuffing
Prep: 20 minutes   Bake: 40 minutes

1 cup shredded carrots	8 cups dry bread cubes
1 cup chopped celery	2 cups finely chopped peeled apples
½ cup chopped onion (1 medium)	½ cup chopped walnuts
½ cup margarine or butter	¼ cup toasted wheat germ
¼ teaspoon ground nutmeg	½ to 1 cup chicken broth

Cook carrots, celery, and onion in hot margarine until tender. Stir in nutmeg, ¼ teaspoon salt, and ¼ teaspoon pepper.

In a large bowl combine bread cubes, apples, nuts, and wheat germ; add carrot mixture. Drizzle with enough of the broth to moisten, tossing lightly. Place stuffing in a 3-quart casserole. Cover and bake in a 325° oven for 40 to 45 minutes or until heated through. Makes about 11 cups (12 to 14 servings).

Nutrition facts per serving: 221 calories, **12 g** total fat (**3 g** saturated fat), **0 mg** cholesterol, **363 mg** sodium, **24 g** carbohydrate, **1 g** fiber, **5 g** protein

Pennsylvania Red Cabbage
Start to finish: 15 minutes

2 tablespoons brown sugar	¼ teaspoon caraway seed
2 tablespoons vinegar	2 cups shredded red or green cabbage
2 tablespoons water	¾ cup coarsely chopped apple (1 small)
1 tablespoon cooking oil	

In a large skillet combine the brown sugar, vinegar, water, oil, caraway seed, ¼ teaspoon salt, and dash pepper. Cook for 2 to 3 minutes or until hot, stirring occasionally. Stir in the cabbage and apple. Cover and cook over medium-low heat about 5 minutes or until cabbage is crisp-tender, stirring occasionally. Makes 3 or 4 servings.

Nutrition facts per serving: 90 calories, **5 g** total fat (**1 g** saturated fat), **0 mg** cholesterol, **184 mg** sodium, **13 g** carbohydrate, **2 g** fiber, **1 g** protein

Sweet-sour cabbage 1940s' style required the cabbage to be simmered in 2 cups of water. Today, to keep the cabbage crisp-tender, we quickly steam, rather than simmer it.

 Baked Bean Quintet
Prep: 10 minutes   Bake: 1 hour

1 cup chopped onion (1 large)	1 15-ounce can butter beans, drained
6 slices bacon, cut up	1 15-ounce can garbanzo beans, drained
1 clove garlic, minced	¾ cup catsup
1 16-ounce can lima beans, drained	½ cup molasses
1 16-ounce can pork and beans in tomato sauce	¼ cup packed brown sugar
1 15½-ounce can red kidney beans, drained	1 tablespoon prepared mustard
	1 tablespoon Worcestershire sauce

In a skillet cook onion, bacon, and garlic until bacon is done and onion is tender; drain. In bowl combine onion mixture, all beans, catsup, molasses, brown sugar, mustard, and Worcestershire sauce. Transfer to a 3-quart casserole. Bake, covered, in a 375° oven for 1 hour. Makes 12 to 16 servings.

Crockery-cooker directions: Prepare bean mixture as above. Transfer to a 3½- or 4-quart electric crockery cooker. Cover and cook on low-heat setting for 10 to 12 hours or on high-heat setting for 4 to 5 hours.

Nutrition facts per serving: 236 calories, **3 g** total fat (**1 g** saturated fat), **5 mg** cholesterol, **768 mg** sodium, **46 g** carbohydrate, **8 g** fiber, **11 g** protein

Because they've been an American staple since Colonial days, baked beans were a shoo-in for a place in our 1930 cookbook—but the recipe used kidney beans, not navy or white beans. By the second edition, a more traditional version appeared. Today, we offer three different bean recipes, including this 1980s' spin-off that gives you the option of making them in the oven or crockery cooker. Take them along the next time you're invited to a potluck.

Lemony Fettuccine Alfredo
with Peas (see below)

*A must on almost every
Italian restaurant menu,
this quick-to-fix pasta
dish first appeared
on our pages in 1989.
Serve it as a side dish
in place of potatoes,
or add some cooked
chicken or ham and
turn it into a main dish.*

Fettuccine Alfredo
Start to finish: 35 minutes

⅓ cup half-and-half, light cream, or whipping cream	4 ounces dried spinach or plain fettuccine
1 tablespoon margarine or butter	⅓ cup finely shredded Parmesan cheese
	Cracked black pepper
	Ground nutmeg

Allow half-and-half and margarine or butter to stand at room temperature 30 minutes.

Meanwhile, cook fettuccine according to package directions for 8 to 10 minutes or until tender but still firm. Drain. Return fettuccine to warm saucepan; add half-and-half, margarine or butter, and Parmesan cheese. Toss gently until fettuccine is well coated. Transfer to a warm serving dish. Sprinkle with pepper and nutmeg. Serve immediately. Makes 4 servings.

Lemony Fettuccine Alfredo with Peas: Prepare as above, except add ½ cup frozen peas to the fettuccine for the last 5 minutes of cooking time. Drain well. Return fettuccine and peas to warm saucepan. Add ½ teaspoon finely shredded lemon peel along with the half-and-half, margarine or butter, and Parmesan cheese. Toss gently; transfer to a warm serving dish. Omit pepper and nutmeg. If desired, sprinkle with additional Parmesan cheese.

Nutrition facts per serving: 203 calories, **8 g** total fat (**4 g** saturated fat), **14 mg** cholesterol, **198 mg** sodium, **24 g** carbohydrate, **0 g** fiber, **8 g** protein
Nutrition facts per serving Lemony Fettuccine Alfredo with Peas: 214 calories, **8 g** total fat (**4 g** saturated fat)

Wilted Spinach Salad

Start to finish: 25 minutes

6 cups torn fresh spinach or romaine	3 tablespoons vinegar
1 cup sliced fresh mushrooms	1 teaspoon sugar
	¼ teaspoon dry mustard
¼ cup thinly sliced green onions (2)	1 cup sliced fresh strawberries
3 slices bacon	1 hard-cooked egg, chopped

In a large bowl combine spinach, mushrooms, and green onions. If desired, sprinkle with pepper; set aside.

For dressing, in a 12-inch skillet cook bacon until crisp. Remove bacon, reserving 2 tablespoons drippings in skillet. (Or, if desired, substitute 2 tablespoons salad oil for bacon drippings.) Crumble bacon; set aside. Stir vinegar, sugar, and dry mustard into drippings. Bring to boiling; remove from heat. Add the spinach mixture. Toss mixture in skillet for 30 to 60 seconds or until spinach is just wilted.

Transfer to a serving dish. Add strawberries. Top salad with egg and bacon. Serve immediately. Makes 4 servings.

Nutrition facts per serving: 86 calories, **4 g** total fat (**1 g** saturated fat), **57 mg** cholesterol, **159 mg** sodium, **8 g** carbohydrate, **3 g** fiber, **6 g** protein

In our 1941 edition we paid homage to this recipe's German roots by labeling it Pennsylvania Dutch Spinach. Today's version is a creative adaptation featuring fresh mushrooms, green onions, and strawberries in addition to the spinach.

Three-Bean Salad

Prep: 15 minutes   Chill: 4 to 24 hours

1 16-ounce can cut wax beans, one 16-ounce can lima beans, or one 15-ounce can garbanzo beans	½ cup chopped onion (1 medium)
	½ cup chopped green sweet pepper
	½ cup vinegar
1 8-ounce can cut green beans or one 8-ounce can black beans	¼ cup salad oil
	2 tablespoons sugar
	½ teaspoon celery seed
1 8-ounce can red kidney beans	½ teaspoon dry mustard
	1 clove garlic, minced

Rinse and drain all the beans. In a large bowl combine all beans, onion, and sweet pepper. For dressing, in a screw-top jar combine the vinegar, oil, sugar, celery seed, dry mustard, and garlic. Cover and shake well. Pour over vegetables; stir lightly. Cover and chill in refrigerator for at least 4 hours or up to 24 hours, stirring often. Makes 6 servings.

Nutrition facts per serving: 72 calories, **2 g** total fat (**0 g** saturated fat), **0 mg** cholesterol, **201 mg** sodium, **11 g** carbohydrate, **3 g** fiber, **3 g** protein

This chilled bean medley first surfaced in the 1960s and was tremendously popular because it was so easy to make. Even the earliest version only required the cook to open 3 cans of beans, chop a few vegetables, and add a vinaigrette-style dressing.

Make-ahead convenience made this layered salad a darling of the late 1970s and early 1980s. Then as now, you could chill this salad up to 24 hours. In fact, holding the salad overnight improves the flavor.

 24-Hour Vegetable Salad

Prep: 30 minutes   Chill: 2 to 24 hours

4 **cups torn iceberg lettuce, romaine, leaf lettuce, Bibb lettuce, and/or fresh spinach**	¾ **cup shredded Swiss, American, or cheddar cheese (3 ounces)**
1 **cup sliced fresh mushrooms, broccoli flowerets, or frozen peas**	¼ **cup thinly sliced green onions (2)**
1 **cup shredded carrots (2 medium)**	¾ **cup mayonnaise or salad dressing**
2 **hard-cooked eggs, sliced**	1½ **teaspoons lemon juice**
6 **slices bacon, crisp-cooked, drained, and crumbled (¼ pound)**	½ **teaspoon dried dillweed (optional)**
	Thinly sliced green onions (optional)

Place lettuce in a 3-quart salad bowl. If desired, sprinkle with salt and pepper. Layer mushrooms, broccoli, or peas atop lettuce. Then, layer in the following order: carrots, eggs, bacon, ½ cup of the cheese, and the ¼ cup green onions.

For dressing, in small bowl combine the mayonnaise or salad dressing, lemon juice, and, if desired, dillweed. Spread dressing over salad, sealing to edge of bowl. Sprinkle with the remaining cheese. If desired, garnish with additional green onion. Cover; chill in refrigerator for at least 2 hours or up to 24 hours. Before serving, toss to coat vegetables. Serves 6 to 8.

Nutrition facts per serving: 330 calories, **31 g** total fat (**7 g** saturated fat), **105 mg** cholesterol, **326 mg** sodium, **5 g** carbohydrate, **1 g** fiber, **9 g** protein

Macaroni Salad
Prep: 30 minutes   Chill: 4 to 24 hours

1 cup dried elbow macaroni or wagon-wheel macaroni (3 ounces)	2 tablespoons thinly sliced green onion or chopped onion
¾ cup cubed cheddar or American cheese (3 ounces)	½ cup mayonnaise or salad dressing
½ cup thinly sliced celery (1 stalk)	¼ cup sweet or dill pickle relish or chopped sweet or dill pickles
½ cup frozen peas	2 tablespoons milk
½ cup thinly sliced radishes	¼ teaspoon salt
	Dash pepper
	2 hard-cooked eggs, coarsely chopped
	Milk (optional)

Cook pasta according to package directions. Drain pasta. Rinse with cold water; drain again. In a large mixing bowl combine cooked pasta, cheese, celery, peas, radishes, and green onion.

For dressing, in a small bowl stir together mayonnaise or salad dressing, pickle relish or pickles, the 2 tablespoons milk, the salt, and pepper.

Pour dressing over pasta mixture. Add chopped eggs. Toss lightly to coat. Cover and chill in the refrigerator for at least 4 hours or up to 24 hours. Before serving, if necessary, stir in additional milk to moisten. Makes 6 servings.

Nutrition facts per serving: 298 calories, **22 g** total fat (**6 g** saturated fat), **97 mg** cholesterol, **409 mg** sodium, **18 g** carbohydrate, **1 g** fiber, **9 g** protein

As a trip through any restaurant buffet line proves, this creamy pasta salad is perennially popular. We've dressed up the 1950s' version by adding peas and sliced radishes. You can make the flavor of your salad sweet or sour by using either sweet or dill pickle relish or pickles.

In our 1930 cookbook, we recommended cooks serve Thousand Island Dressing over hearts of lettuce, vegetable or gelatin salads, or as a tartar sauce for fish. Today we're more likely to use this zesty dressing with tossed salads or as a sandwich spread.

 1930

Thousand Island Dressing
Start to finish: 20 minutes

1 cup mayonnaise or salad dressing	1 teaspoon Worcestershire sauce or prepared horseradish (optional)
¼ cup chili sauce	
2 tablespoons finely chopped pimiento-stuffed olives	
	1 hard-cooked egg, finely chopped
2 tablespoons finely chopped green or red sweet pepper	1 to 2 tablespoons milk (optional)
2 tablespoons finely chopped onion	

In small bowl combine mayonnaise or salad dressing and chili sauce. Stir in olives, sweet pepper, onion, Worcestershire sauce or prepared horseradish (if desired), and hard-cooked egg.

Serve immediately or cover and store in refrigerator for up to 1 week. Before serving, if necessary, stir in enough of the milk to make dressing of desired consistency. Makes 1½ cups.

Nutrition facts per tablespoon: 73 calories, **8 g** total fat (**1 g** saturated fat), **14 mg** cholesterol, **104 mg** sodium, **1 g** carbohydrate, **0 g** fiber, **1 g** protein

Although this dressing was created in the 1920s in honor of a play called The Green Goddess, *our first version didn't appear until the cookbook's 1953 edition. It was served over a unique arranged salad of romaine, leaf lettuce, Belgian endive, tomatoes, beets, and shrimp.*

1953

Green Goddess Dressing
Start to finish: 15 minutes

¾ cup packed fresh parsley sprigs	1 teaspoon anchovy paste or 1 anchovy fillet, cut up
⅓ cup mayonnaise or salad dressing	
	¼ teaspoon dried basil, crushed
⅓ cup dairy sour cream or plain yogurt	⅛ teaspoon garlic powder
1 green onion, cut up	⅛ teaspoon dried tarragon, crushed
1 tablespoon vinegar	1 to 2 tablespoons milk

In a blender container or food processor bowl combine parsley, mayonnaise or salad dressing, sour cream or yogurt, green onion, vinegar, anchovy paste or anchovy, basil, garlic powder, and tarragon. Cover and blend or process until smooth.

Serve immediately or cover and store in refrigerator for up to 2 weeks. Before serving, stir in enough of the milk to make dressing of desired consistency. Makes about 1 cup.

Nutrition facts per tablespoon: 45 calories, **5 g** total fat (**1 g** saturated fat), **5 mg** cholesterol, **40 mg** sodium, **1 g** carbohydrate, **0 g** fiber, **0 g** protein

breads

Cinnamon
Swirl Bread (see
opposite page)

*This rich dough, called
Basic Sweet Dough in
the first edition of our
cookbook, has been
reformulated over the
years to use less sugar.
Here we've transformed
it into three distinctly
different loaves.*

 Egg Bread
Prep: 30 minutes   Rise: 1½ hours   Bake: 25 minutes

4¾ to 5¼ cups all-purpose
      flour
  1 package active dry
      yeast
1⅓ cups milk

  3 tablespoons sugar
  3 tablespoons butter
  ½ teaspoon salt
  2 eggs

In a large mixing bowl stir together 2 cups of the flour and
the yeast; set aside. In a medium saucepan heat and stir milk,
sugar, butter, and salt just until warm (120° to 130°) and
butter almost melts. Add milk mixture to flour mixture along
with the eggs. Beat with an electric mixer on low to medium
speed for 30 seconds, scraping the side of the bowl constantly.
Beat on high speed for 3 minutes. Using a wooden spoon, stir
in as much of the remaining flour as you can.

Turn dough out onto a lightly floured surface. Knead in
enough of the remaining flour to make a moderately stiff
dough that is smooth and elastic (6 to 8 minutes total). Shape
the dough into a ball. Place in a lightly greased bowl, turning

once to grease surface of the dough. Cover and let rise in a warm place until double in size (about 1 hour).

Punch dough down. Turn dough onto a lightly floured surface. Divide dough in half. Cover and let rest for 10 minutes. Lightly grease two 8×4×2-inch loaf pans.

Shape each portion of dough into a loaf by patting or rolling.* Place dough in prepared pans. Cover and let rise in a warm place until nearly double (about 30 minutes).

Bake in a 375° oven for 25 to 30 minutes or until bread sounds hollow when you tap the top. If necessary, to prevent overbrowning, cover loosely with foil for the last 10 minutes of baking. Remove bread from pans. Cool on wire racks. Makes 2 loaves (32 servings).

Cinnamon Swirl Bread: Prepare Egg Bread as on opposite page, except instead of shaping into loaves, on a floured surface roll each portion of dough into a 12×7-inch rectangle. Brush lightly with water. Combine ½ cup sugar and 2 teaspoons ground cinnamon. Sprinkle half of the sugar-cinnamon mixture over each rectangle. Roll up, jelly-roll style, starting from a short side. Pinch seam and ends to seal. Place seam side down in prepared loaf pans. Rise and bake as directed. If desired, for icing, combine 1 cup sifted powdered sugar, 1 tablespoon milk, and ¼ teaspoon vanilla; stir in additional milk, 1 teaspoon at a time, until drizzling consistency. Drizzle over warm loaves.

Challah: Prepare Egg Bread as on opposite page, except substitute 1¼ cups water for the milk and pareve margarine for butter. Prepare as directed through the first rising. Punch dough down; divide in thirds. Cover; let rest 10 minutes. Roll each third into an 18-inch-long rope. Place ropes on a large baking sheet 1 inch apart; braid. Cover; let rise 30 minutes or until nearly double. Brush braid with 1 beaten egg yolk and sprinkle with 2 teaspoons poppy seed. Bake as directed. Makes 1 braid (32 servings).

*Note: To shape dough, gently pat each half into a loaf, pinching and tucking the edges beneath the loaf. Or, roll each half of dough into a 12×8-inch rectangle. Tightly roll up, jelly-roll style, starting from a short side. Pinch seam to seal.

Nutrition facts per serving: 87 calories, **2 g** total fat (**1 g** saturated fat), **19 mg** cholesterol, **72 mg** sodium, **15 g** carbohydrate, **1 g** fiber, **3 g** protein
Nutrition facts per serving Cinnamon Swirl Bread: 99 calories, **2 g** total fat (**1 g** saturated fat)
Nutrition facts per serving Challah: 83 calories, **2 g** total fat (**0 g** saturated fat)

Potato Rolls

Prep: 45 minutes   Rise: 1¾ hours   Bake: 10 minutes

4 to 4½ cups all-purpose flour	¼ cup sugar
	¼ cup shortening
1 package active dry yeast	1½ teaspoons salt
	1 beaten egg
1 cup milk	½ cup mashed potato*
¼ cup water	

In a large mixing bowl stir together 2 cups of the flour and the yeast. In a medium saucepan heat and stir milk, water, sugar, shortening, and salt just until warm (120° to 130°) and shortening almost melts. Add milk mixture to flour mixture along with the egg and mashed potato. Beat with an electric mixer on low to medium speed for 30 seconds, scraping side of bowl constantly. Beat on high speed for 3 minutes. Using a wooden spoon, stir in as much of the remaining flour as you can.

Turn dough out onto a lightly floured surface. Knead in enough of the remaining flour to make a moderately stiff dough that is smooth and elastic (6 to 8 minutes total). Shape the dough into a ball. Place in a lightly greased bowl; turn once to grease surface. Cover; let rise in a warm place until nearly double in size (about 1 hour).

Punch dough down. Turn dough out onto a lightly floured surface. Divide dough in half. Cover; let rest for 10 minutes. Meanwhile, lightly grease a baking sheet. Divide each portion of dough into 12 pieces. To shape, gently pull each dough piece into a ball, tucking edges beneath. Place the shaped dough pieces on the prepared baking sheet. Cover; let rise in a warm place until nearly double (about 45 minutes).

Bake in a 400° oven for 10 to 12 minutes or until golden brown. Remove rolls from baking sheet. Cool on a rack. Makes 24 rolls.

Note: Peel and quarter 1 medium potato. In covered saucepan cook in a small amount of boiling lightly salted water for 20 to 25 minutes or until tender; drain. Mash with a potato masher or beat with an electric mixer on low speed. Measure ½ cup.

Nutrition facts per roll: 110 calories, **3 g** total fat (**1 g** saturated fat), **10 mg** cholesterol, **142 mg** sodium, **18 g** carbohydrate, **1 g** fiber, **3 g** protein

Cinnamon Crisps

Prep: 40 minutes   Rise: 1½ hours   Bake: 10 minutes

3½	to 4 cups all-purpose flour	½	cup packed brown sugar
1	package active dry yeast	½	cup butter or margarine, melted
1¼	cups milk	½	teaspoon ground cinnamon
¼	cup granulated sugar	1	cup granulated sugar
¼	cup shortening	½	cup chopped pecans
1	teaspoon salt	1	teaspoon ground cinnamon
1	egg		
½	cup granulated sugar		

In a large mixing bowl combine 2 cups of the flour and the yeast. Heat milk, the ¼ cup granulated sugar, the shortening, and salt just until warm (120° to 130°) and shortening almost melts. Add to flour mixture; add egg. Beat with an electric mixer on low speed for 30 seconds, scraping side of bowl constantly. Beat 3 minutes on high speed. Using a wooden spoon, stir in as much of the remaining flour as you can.

Turn dough out onto a lightly floured surface. Knead in enough of the remaining flour to make a moderately soft dough that is smooth and elastic (3 to 5 minutes total). Shape into a ball. Place in a lightly greased bowl; turn once to grease surface. Cover; let rise in a warm place until double (1 to 1½ hours).

Punch down; divide in half. Cover; let rest 10 minutes. Grease baking sheets; set aside. Roll each dough half into a 12-inch square. Combine the ½ cup granulated sugar, the brown sugar, half of the melted butter or margarine, and the ½ teaspoon ground cinnamon; spread half of the mixture over each square. Roll up, jelly-roll style, starting from a long side; seal seams. Cut each into 12 slices. Place, cut sides down, on prepared baking sheets 3 to 4 inches apart. Flatten each slice to about 3 inches in diameter.

Cover; let rise until nearly double (about 30 minutes). Cover with waxed paper. Using a rolling pin, roll to ⅛-inch thickness; remove paper. Brush rolls with remaining melted butter or margarine. Combine the 1 cup granulated sugar, the pecans, and the 1 teaspoon cinnamon. Sprinkle over rolls. Cover with waxed paper; roll flat again. Remove paper. Bake in a 400° oven 10 to 12 minutes or until golden brown. Immediately transfer to wire racks; cool. Makes 24 crisps.

Nutrition facts per crisp: 209 calories, **8 g** total fat (**3 g** saturated fat), **20 mg** cholesterol, **138 mg** sodium, **32 g** carbohydrate, **1 g** fiber, **3 g** protein

What are Cinnamon Crisps? Think of the best cinnamon roll you have ever eaten; then imagine what it might be like as a cookie—a really big cookie with a crispy-crunchy outside and sweet and chewy inside. That's how we would describe these cinnamon-scented treats.

 Caramel-Nut Rolls
Prep: 25 minutes
Rise: 1½ hours
Bake: 20 minutes

4 to 4⅓ cups all-purpose
   flour
1 package active dry
   yeast
1 cup milk
⅓ cup sugar
⅓ cup butter
½ teaspoon salt
2 eggs
1 recipe Caramel Topping
   (see below)
⅔ cup chopped pecans
3 tablespoons butter,
   melted
½ cup sugar
1 teaspoon ground
   cinnamon

Whether at family get-togethers, county fairs, or national bake-offs, generations of cooks have prided themselves on the quality of their caramel rolls (called Butterscotch Rolls in the first edition of our cookbook). You can lay claim to your own bragging rights when you try your hand at these scrumptious rolls that are Better Homes and Gardens best.

In large bowl combine 2 cups of the flour and yeast; set aside. In saucepan heat and stir milk, the ⅓ cup sugar, the ⅓ cup butter, and salt just until warm (120° to 130°); add to flour mixture along with eggs. Beat with electric mixer on low speed 30 seconds, scraping bowl. Beat on high speed for 3 minutes. Stir in as much of the remaining flour as you can.

Turn dough onto a floured surface. Knead in enough of the remaining flour to make a moderately soft dough that is smooth and elastic (3 to 5 minutes total). Shape into a ball. Place dough in lightly greased bowl; turn once. Cover and let rise in a warm place until double (about 1 hour).

Punch dough down. Turn onto a lightly floured surface. Divide in half. Cover and let rest 10 minutes. Divide Caramel Topping between two 9×1½-inch round baking pans. Sprinkle pecans in pans; set aside.

Roll each dough portion into a 12×8-inch rectangle. Brush the 3 tablespoons melted butter over dough. Combine the ½ cup sugar and the cinnamon; sprinkle over dough. Roll up, jelly-roll style, starting from a long side; seal seam. Cut each into 12 slices. Place in prepared pans. Cover and let rise in a warm place until nearly double (about 30 minutes).

Bake in a 375° oven for 20 to 25 minutes or until golden. Immediately invert baked rolls from pans. Makes 24 rolls.

Caramel Topping: In small saucepan heat and stir ⅔ cup packed brown sugar, ¼ cup butter, and 2 tablespoons light-colored corn syrup until combined.

Nutrition facts per roll: 209 calories, **9 g** total fat (**4 g** saturated fat), **34 mg** cholesterol, **118 mg** sodium, **30 g** carbohydrate, **1 g** fiber, **3 g** protein

Chocolate Swirl Coffee Cake
Prep: 35 minutes   Rise: 2½ hours   Bake: 45 minutes

4 to 4½ cups all-purpose
   flour
2 packages active dry
   yeast
¾ cup sugar
⅔ cup water
½ cup butter, cut up
⅓ cup evaporated milk
½ teaspoon salt

4 egg yolks
¾ cup semisweet chocolate
   pieces
⅓ cup evaporated milk
2 tablespoons sugar
½ teaspoon ground
   cinnamon
   Streusel (see below)

In a large mixing bowl stir together 1½ cups of the flour and the yeast; set aside. In a medium saucepan heat and stir the ¾ cup sugar, the water, butter, ⅓ cup evaporated milk, and salt just until warm (120° to 130°) and butter almost melts. Add milk mixture to flour mixture along with egg yolks. Beat with an electric mixer on low speed for 30 seconds, scraping the side of bowl constantly. Beat on high speed for 3 minutes. Using a wooden spoon, stir in as much of the remaining flour as you can.

Turn dough out onto a lightly floured surface. Knead in enough of the remaining flour to make a moderately soft dough that is smooth and elastic (3 to 5 minutes total). Shape dough into a ball. Place in a lightly greased bowl, turning once to grease surface. Cover and let rise in a warm place until double (about 1½ hours).

Punch dough down. Turn dough onto a lightly floured surface. Cover; let rest for 10 minutes.

Meanwhile, in a small saucepan combine chocolate pieces, ⅓ cup evaporated milk, the 2 tablespoons sugar, and the cinnamon. Cook and stir over low heat until chocolate is melted. Remove from heat; cool.

Grease a 10-inch tube pan; set aside. Roll dough into an 18×10-inch rectangle. Spread chocolate mixture to within 1 inch of edges. Roll up, jelly-roll style, starting from a long side. Pinch seam and ends to seal. Place, seam side down, in prepared pan. Sprinkle Streusel over dough in pan. Cover and let rise in a warm place until nearly double (about 1 hour).

Bake in a 350° oven for 45 to 50 minutes or until coffee cake sounds hollow when lightly tapped. Cool in pan on a wire rack for 15 minutes. Remove from pan. Cool on a wire rack. If desired, serve warm. Makes 12 to 16 servings.

Streusel: In a small bowl combine ¼ cup all-purpose flour, ¼ cup sugar, and 1 teaspoon ground cinnamon. Cut in ¼ cup butter until mixture resembles coarse crumbs. Stir in ¼ cup chopped walnuts or pecans.

Nutrition facts per serving: 429 calories, **19 g** total fat (**8 g** saturated fat), **106 mg** cholesterol, **224 mg** sodium, **60 g** carbohydrate, **2 g** fiber, **8 g** protein

We've published quite a few coffee cake recipes since 1930, and this is one that made the hit parade. This coffee cake is unusual in that it is yeast-risen, which makes it fluffy. Setting it apart from the rest is its chocolate filling, which gets a flavor boost from a touch of cinnamon.

Waffles were all the rage in the 1930s, and not just for breakfast either. "Waffle suppers" were popular, as were waffles for lunch. Our Chocolate-Nut Waffles, however, make a fantastic dessert course. And to really do it right, be sure to embellish each with a generous dollop of sweetened whipped cream.

 ### Chocolate-Nut Waffles

Prep: 15 minutes   Bake: Per manufacturer's directions

1¾ cups all-purpose flour	2 ounces semisweet chocolate, melted
½ cup sugar	
4 teaspoons baking powder	1 teaspoon vanilla
½ teaspoon salt	½ cup chopped walnuts
2 egg yolks	2 egg whites
1½ cups milk	Sweetened whipped cream (optional)
½ cup shortening, melted	

In a medium mixing bowl stir together flour, sugar, baking powder, and salt. Make a well in the center of mixture; set aside.

In another medium mixing bowl beat egg yolks slightly. Stir in milk, shortening, chocolate, and vanilla. Add chocolate mixture all at once to flour mixture. Stir until just moistened (batter should be lumpy). Stir in nuts.

In a small mixing bowl beat egg whites until stiff peaks form (tips stand straight). Gently fold beaten egg whites into flour-chocolate mixture, leaving a few fluffs of egg white. Do not overmix.

Pour 1 to 1¼ cups batter onto grids of a preheated, lightly greased waffle baker. Close lid quickly; do not open until done. Bake according to manufacturer's directions. When done, use a fork to lift waffle off grid. Repeat with remaining batter. If desired, serve warm with whipped cream. Makes 12 to 16 (4-inch) waffles.

Nutrition facts per waffle: 253 calories, **15 g** total fat (**4 g** saturated fat), **38 mg** cholesterol, **237 mg** sodium, **27 g** carbohydrate, **1 g** fiber, **5 g** protein

Gingerbread Waffles
Prep: 15 minutes   Bake: Per manufacturer's directions

¼ **cup sugar**
¼ **cup shortening**
1 **egg**
½ **cup molasses**
1¼ **cups all-purpose flour**
¾ **teaspoon baking soda**
¼ **teaspoon salt**

1 **teaspoon ground ginger**
½ **teaspoon ground cinnamon**
¼ **teaspoon ground cloves**
½ **cup hot water**

In a medium mixing bowl beat sugar and shortening together until fluffy. Add egg and molasses; beat until combined. Combine the flour, baking soda, salt, ginger, cinnamon, and cloves. Add to sugar mixture; beat until smooth. Stir in the hot water.

Pour 1 to 1¼ cups batter onto grids of a preheated, lightly greased waffle baker. Close lid quickly; do not open until done. Bake according to manufacturer's directions. Do not overbake. When done, use a fork to lift waffle off grid. Repeat with remaining batter. Makes 8 (4-inch) waffles.

Nutrition facts per waffle: 207 calories, **7 g** total fat (**2 g** saturated fat), **27 mg** cholesterol, **197 mg** sodium, **33 g** carbohydrate, **0 g** fiber, **3 g** protein

Ginger Muffins
Prep: 20 minutes   Bake: 20 minutes

1½ **cups all-purpose flour**
¾ **teaspoon baking soda**
½ **teaspoon ground cinnamon**
½ **teaspoon ground ginger**

¼ **teaspoon ground cloves**
¼ **cup sugar**
¼ **cup shortening**
1 **egg**
½ **cup mild-flavored molasses**

Grease twelve 2½-inch muffin cups or line them with paper bake cups; set aside.

In a small mixing bowl combine flour, baking soda, cinnamon, ginger, cloves, and ¼ teaspoon salt; set aside. In a medium mixing bowl beat together sugar and shortening until fluffy. Add egg and molasses; beat until combined. Add flour mixture; beat until well mixed. Gradually add ½ cup hot water, mixing just until smooth. Spoon batter into prepared muffin cups, filling each two-thirds full.

Bake in a 375° oven about 20 minutes or until a toothpick comes out clean. Cool in muffin cups on wire rack for 5 minutes. Remove from cups; cool on rack. Makes 12 muffins.

Nutrition facts per muffin: 147 calories, **5 g** total fat (**1 g** saturated fat), **18 mg** cholesterol, **131 mg** sodium, **24 g** carbohydrate, **0 g** fiber, **2 g** protein

In the '30s, people were making waffles out of all sorts of novelty ingredients. (Have you ever tried a pea pulp waffle?) These Gingerbread Waffles, on the other hand, have withstood the test of time. For dessert, serve them with sweetened whipped cream. And for breakfast, there's no need to break with tradition—you'll love 'em with butter and maple syrup!

Have you noticed that muffins have gotten bigger over the years? Not only that, the texture has gone soft and sort of cakey as well. Testing this recipe reminded us of how nice muffins used to be when they came in a smaller size and with a slightly coarser texture. The crust even crunches a bit when you bite into it.

Zucchini, a West Coast fad in the 1930s, first showed up in Better Homes and Gardens *magazine in 1937, but it wasn't generally served outside the states of Washington and California until the late 1940s. By the 1970s and 1980s, however, zucchini was so common cooks were looking for ways to use up the prolific vegetable. This family-pleasing quick bread from our 1981 edition was our innovative solution to the zucchini 'problem.'*

Zucchini Bread
Prep: 15 minutes   Bake: 55 minutes

1½ cups all-purpose flour
1   teaspoon ground
     cinnamon
½   teaspoon baking soda
¼   teaspoon baking
     powder
¼   teaspoon salt
¼   teaspoon ground
     nutmeg

1   cup sugar
1   cup finely shredded,
     unpeeled zucchini
¼   cup cooking oil
1   egg
¼   teaspoon finely
     shredded lemon peel
½   cup chopped walnuts
     or pecans

Grease bottom and ½ inch up sides of an 8×4×2-inch loaf pan; set aside. In a medium mixing bowl combine the flour, cinnamon, baking soda, baking powder, salt, and nutmeg; set aside.

In another medium mixing bowl combine sugar, shredded zucchini, cooking oil, egg, and lemon peel; mix well. Add flour mixture to zucchini mixture. Stir just until moistened (batter should be lumpy). Fold in walnuts or pecans.

Spoon batter into the prepared pan. Bake in a 350° oven 55 to 60 minutes or until a toothpick inserted near center comes out clean. Cool in the pan on a wire rack for 10 minutes. Remove loaf from pan. Cool completely on the wire rack. Wrap and store overnight. Makes 1 loaf (16 servings).

Apple Bread: Prepare as above, except substitute 1 cup finely shredded, peeled apple for the shredded zucchini. Continue as directed.

Nutrition facts per serving: 148 calories, **6 g** total fat (**1 g** saturated fat), **13 mg** cholesterol, **83 mg** sodium, **22 g** carbohydrate, **1 g** fiber, **2 g** protein
    Nutrition facts per serving Apple Bread: 151 calories, **6 g** total fat (**1 g** saturated fat)

 **Fruit Coffee Cake**
Prep: 30 minutes
Bake: 40 minutes

1½ **cups desired fruit***
¼ **cup water**
1¼ **cups sugar**
2 **tablespoons cornstarch**
1¾ **cups all-purpose flour**
½ **teaspoon baking powder**
¼ **teaspoon baking soda**
¼ **cup butter**
1 **beaten egg**
½ **cup buttermilk or sour milk****
½ **teaspoon vanilla**
2 **tablespoons butter**

In a medium saucepan combine fruit and water. Bring to boiling; reduce heat. Cover and simmer for 5 minutes or until fruit is tender. Combine ¼ cup of the sugar and the cornstarch; stir into fruit. Cook and stir over medium heat until mixture is thickened and bubbly. Cook and stir 2 minutes more; set aside.

In a mixing bowl combine 1½ cups of the flour, baking powder, baking soda, and ¾ cup of the remaining sugar. Cut in the ¼ cup butter until mixture resembles coarse crumbs. Make a well in the center of the flour mixture; set aside.

In another bowl combine egg, buttermilk or sour milk, and vanilla. Add egg mixture all at once to flour mixture. Using a fork, stir just until moistened (batter should be lumpy). Spread half of the batter into an ungreased 8×8×2-inch baking pan. Spread fruit mixture over batter. Drop remaining batter in small mounds atop filling.

Stir together remaining flour and remaining sugar. Cut in the 2 tablespoons butter until mixture resembles coarse crumbs. Sprinkle atop coffee cake. Bake in a 350° oven for 40 to 45 minutes or until golden. Serve warm. Serves 9.

Note: Use blueberries or chopped peeled apple, apricots, peaches, or pineapple. Or, use red raspberries, except omit simmering.

**Note:* To make sour milk, place 1½ teaspoons lemon juice in 1-cup glass measuring cup. Add enough milk to make ½ cup total liquid; stir. Let mixture stand for 5 minutes before using.

Nutrition facts per serving: 268 calories, **9 g** total fat (**2 g** saturated fat), **24 mg** cholesterol, **167 mg** sodium, **45 g** carbohydrate, **1 g** fiber, **4 g** protein

Fruit-filled coffee cakes have appeared in our cookbooks since the 1940s, but this extraordinary quick bread made its first appearance in 1981 as Any Fruit Coffee Cake. The title said it all, as you have your choice of blueberries, apple, apricots, peaches, or pineapple.

When this breakfast treat appeared in our 1937 cookbook, it was called Cowboy Cake. Although the name has been changed, this coffee cake's great taste and texture have stayed the same.

 Buttermilk Coffee Cake
Prep: 20 minutes   Bake: 35 minutes

2½ cups all-purpose flour	½ teaspoon ground
1½ cups packed brown	cinnamon
sugar	½ teaspoon ground
½ teaspoon salt	nutmeg
⅔ cup butter or	2 beaten eggs
shortening	1⅓ cups buttermilk
2 teaspoons baking	or sour milk*
powder	½ cup chopped nuts
½ teaspoon baking soda	

Grease bottom and ½ inch up sides of a 13×9×2-inch baking pan; set aside. Combine flour, brown sugar, and salt. Cut in butter or shortening until mixture resembles coarse crumbs; set aside ½ cup. Stir baking powder, baking soda, cinnamon, and nutmeg into remaining crumb mixture.

Combine eggs and buttermilk or sour milk. Add egg mixture all at once to cinnamon-crumb mixture; mix well. Spoon batter into prepared pan. Stir together reserved crumb mixture and nuts. Sprinkle atop batter. Bake in a 350° oven for 35 to 40 minutes or until a toothpick inserted near the center comes out clean. Serve warm. Makes 18 servings.

*Note: To make sour milk, place 4 teaspoons lemon juice in a 2-cup glass measuring cup. Add enough milk to make 1⅓ cups total liquid; stir. Let mixture stand for 5 minutes before using.

Nutrition facts per serving: 214 calories, **10 g** total fat (**2 g** saturated fat), **33 mg** cholesterol, **228 mg** sodium, **28 g** carbohydrate, **1 g** fiber, **3 g** protein

desserts

The novelty of using carrots in cake captivated cooks of the 1960s. What's more, this super-moist cake was oil-based—no messy shortening to measure. Today, this rich, dense cake ranks as a culinary classic. For best results, use a fine shredding surface for the carrots.

 Carrot Cake
Prep: 20 minutes   Bake: 30 minutes   Cool: 2 hours

2 **cups all-purpose flour**	1 **cup cooking oil**
2 **cups sugar**	4 **eggs**
1 **teaspoon baking powder**	1 **recipe Cream Cheese Frosting (see opposite page)**
1 **teaspoon baking soda**	**Walnut halves (optional)**
1 **teaspoon ground cinnamon**	**Orange peel strips (optional)**
3 **cups finely shredded carrots**	

Grease and lightly flour two 9×1½-inch round baking pans or grease one 13×9×2-inch baking pan; set pan(s) aside.

In a large mixing bowl combine flour, sugar, baking powder, baking soda, and cinnamon. Add carrots, oil, and eggs. Beat with an electric mixer until combined. Pour batter into the prepared pan(s).

Bake in a 350° oven for 30 to 35 minutes for round pans or 35 to 40 minutes for 13×9-inch pan or until a toothpick comes out clean. Cool layer cakes in pans on wire racks for 10 minutes. Remove from pans. Cool thoroughly on wire racks. Or, place 13×9-inch cake in pan on a wire rack; cool thoroughly. Frost with Cream Cheese Frosting. If desired, garnish with walnut halves and orange peel. Cover and store in refrigerator. Makes 12 to 16 servings.

Pineapple-Carrot Cake: Prepare as above, except drain one 8-ounce can crushed pineapple. Add drained pineapple and ½ cup coconut with the shredded carrot.

Nutrition facts per serving (with frosting): 650 calories, **33 g** total fat (**11 g** saturated fat), **107 mg** cholesterol, **287 mg** sodium, **89 g** carbohydrate, **1 g** fiber, **5 g** protein
Nutrition facts per serving Pineapple-Carrot Cake (with frosting): 687 calories, **34 g** total fat (**12 g** saturated fat)

 Cream Cheese Frosting
Start to finish: 20 minutes

2 3-ounce packages cream cheese, softened	**2 teaspoons vanilla**
½ cup butter, softened	**4½ to 4¾ cups sifted powdered sugar**

Beat together cream cheese, butter, and vanilla until light and fluffy. Gradually add 2 cups of the powdered sugar, beating well. Gradually beat in enough of the remaining powdered sugar to reach spreading consistency. Makes enough frosting to frost tops and sides of two 8- or 9-inch layers. Cover and store cake in refrigerator.

Nutrition facts per serving (¹⁄₁₂ of recipe): 263 calories, **13 g** total fat (**8 g** saturated fat), **36 mg** cholesterol, **120 mg** sodium, **38 g** carbohydrate, **0 g** fiber, **1 g** protein

Cream Cheese Frosting ranks as a veteran in its field. Long before its classic partner, carrot cake, came along, cooks of the late 1930s and early 1940s were using it to bedeck their favorite cakes and cookies.

Bundt cakes were so popular in the 1980s, everyone was making them, including us. What made them special? Perhaps it was the neat shape or the fact that they always seemed to come out so moist and delicious. Whatever the reason, they're still mighty tasty. Butterscotch Marble Cake was not only one of our first Bundt cakes, it remains one of the best.

1981 Butterscotch Marble Cake
Prep: 20 minutes   Bake: 55 minutes   Cool: 2 hours

1	package 2-layer-size white cake mix	¼	cup cooking oil
1	4-serving-size package instant butterscotch pudding mix	4	eggs
		½	cup chocolate-flavored syrup
			Sifted powdered sugar

Grease and flour a 10-inch fluted tube pan; set aside. In bowl combine cake mix, pudding mix, oil, and eggs. Beat with electric mixer on low speed until mixed. Beat at medium speed for 2 minutes, scraping side of bowl often. Transfer 1½ cups batter to another bowl; stir in chocolate-flavored syrup. Pour light batter into prepared pan. Spoon chocolate batter over. Using knife, gently cut through batters to marble. Bake in 350° oven for 55 to 60 minutes or until a toothpick comes out clean. Cool in pan on wire rack for 15 minutes. Remove from pan; cool completely on rack. Sprinkle with powdered sugar. Serves 12.

Nutrition facts per serving: 306 calories, **9 g** total fat (**2 g** saturated fat), **71 mg** cholesterol, **331 mg** sodium, **52 g** carbohydrate, **1 g** fiber, **4 g** protein

These days, prunes are a little neglected, even though they do add sweet richness and moistness to baked goods. Prune Spice Cake is delectably moist, with just the right spiciness, making it wonderful in the afternoon with a nice hot cup of good tea— or a glass of milk, a cup of coffee, or just about anything, at any time.

1953 Prune Spice Cake
Prep: 15 minutes   Cook: 20 minutes   Bake: 35 minutes

1½	cups dried pitted prunes	¼	teaspoon ground cloves
2	cups all-purpose flour	½	cup cooking oil
1½	cups sugar	3	eggs
1¼	teaspoons baking soda	1	recipe Topping (see below)
1	teaspoon *each* ground cinnamon and nutmeg	½	cup chopped walnuts

Grease and flour a 3-quart rectangular baking dish; set aside. In saucepan cover prunes with water. Heat to boiling; reduce heat. Cover and simmer for 20 minutes or until tender. (Do not sweeten.) Drain, reserving ⅔ cup of the liquid (add water, if necessary). Chop prunes. Mix flour, sugar, soda, cinnamon, nutmeg, cloves, and ¾ teaspoon salt. Add reserved liquid and oil. Beat with an electric mixer on medium speed just until moistened. Add eggs; beat 1 minute more. Stir in prunes.

Pour into prepared baking dish. Sprinkle with Topping and nuts. Bake in 350° oven about 35 minutes or until a toothpick inserted near center comes out clean. Serve warm. Serves 16.

Topping: Combine ½ cup sugar and ¼ cup all-purpose flour. Cut in 2 tablespoons butter until crumbly.

Nutrition facts per serving: 304 calories, **12 g** total fat (**2 g** saturated fat), **44 mg** cholesterol, **226 mg** sodium, **48 g** carbohydrate, **2 g** fiber, **4 g** protein

Graham Cracker Cake
Prep: 45 minutes   Bake: 20 minutes   Chill (filling): 4 hours

3 eggs, separated	½ teaspoon vanilla
1⅔ cups finely crushed graham crackers	¾ cup milk
¼ cup all-purpose flour	½ cup chopped walnuts
1½ teaspoons baking powder	1 recipe Cream Filling (see below)
½ cup shortening	1 recipe Brown Sugar 7-Minute Frosting (see below)
1 cup sugar	

Place egg whites in a bowl; allow to stand at room temperature for 30 minutes. Lightly grease and flour two 8×1½-inch or 9×1½-inch round baking pans; set aside. Combine graham crackers, flour, baking powder, and ¼ teaspoon salt; set aside.

In large bowl beat shortening with an electric mixer on medium speed about 30 seconds. Add sugar and vanilla; beat until combined. Add egg yolks; beat until combined. Add flour mixture and milk alternately to beaten mixture, beating on low to medium speed after each addition just until mixed. Stir in nuts.

Thoroughly wash beaters. Beat egg whites with an electric mixer on high speed until stiff peaks form (tips stand straight). Gently fold whites into batter. Spread into prepared pans. Bake in 350° oven for 20 to 25 minutes or until toothpick inserted near center comes out clean. Cool on wire racks for 10 minutes. Remove from pans. Cool completely on racks.

To assemble, place cake layer on a serving plate; spread with cooled Cream Filling to within ¼ inch of edge. Top with remaining cake layer. Spread side and top with Brown Sugar 7-Minute Frosting. Cover; store in refrigerator. Serves 12.

Cream Filling: In a medium saucepan combine ¼ cup sugar, 2 tablespoons all-purpose flour, and ¼ teaspoon salt. Stir in 1 cup milk. Cook and stir over medium heat until thickened and bubbly. Cook and stir 2 minutes more. Remove from heat. Gradually stir about ½ cup of the hot milk mixture into 2 slightly beaten egg yolks. Stir egg mixture into milk mixture in saucepan. Bring to gentle boil; reduce heat. Cook and stir for 2 minutes more. Remove from heat. Stir in ½ teaspoon vanilla. Pour into a bowl; cover with plastic wrap. Chill thoroughly.

Brown Sugar 7-Minute Frosting: In top of a double boiler mix ¾ cup packed brown sugar, 3 tablespoons cold water, 1 egg white, and ⅛ teaspoon cream of tartar. Beat with electric mixer on low speed for 30 seconds. Place over boiling water (upper pan should not touch water). Cook, beating constantly with the mixer on high speed, about 7 minutes or until stiff peaks form (tips stand straight). Remove from heat; add ½ teaspoon vanilla. Beat 2 to 3 minutes more or until spreading consistency.

Nutrition facts per serving: 346 calories, **15 g** total fat (**4 g** saturated fat), **91 mg** cholesterol, **242 mg** sodium, **47 g** carbohydrate, **1 g** fiber, **6 g** protein

Every element of this cake—from its uniquely textured graham-flavored layers and sumptuous cream filling, to its special 7-minute frosting—tells you that it is something meant for celebrations. In fact, the simple act of preparing it for a few special (and lucky!) people is an experience to be savored. Digging into it is merely the icing on the cake.

Dense, intensely chocolatey, tender, and moist—this baked treat has everything we want in a chocolate cake. Partner it with a fudgy sour cream frosting, and you have a chocolate cake that'll disappear so fast you just might have to make two next time around.

 1989 ## Sour Cream-Chocolate Cake
Prep: 30 minutes   Bake: 30 minutes   Cool: 2 hours

2 **eggs**	3 **ounces unsweetened**
1¾ **cups all-purpose flour**	**chocolate, melted**
1 **teaspoon baking soda**	**and cooled**
¼ **teaspoon salt**	½ **cup dairy sour cream**
½ **cup shortening**	1 **cup cold water**
1½ **cups sugar**	1 **recipe Chocolate-Sour**
½ **teaspoon vanilla**	**Cream Frosting**
	(see below)

Allow eggs to stand at room temperature for 30 minutes. Grease and lightly flour two 8×1½-inch or 9×1½-inch round baking pans. (Or, grease one 13×9×2-inch baking pan.) Set aside.

In a small bowl stir together the flour, baking soda, and salt. In a large mixing bowl beat shortening with an electric mixer on medium speed about 30 seconds. Add the sugar and vanilla. Beat until well combined. Add eggs, 1 at a time, beating for 1 minute after each. Stir in the cooled chocolate and sour cream. Add flour mixture and cold water alternately to beaten mixture, beating on low speed after each addition just until combined. Pour batter into prepared pan(s).

Bake in a 350° oven for 30 to 35 minutes or until top springs back when lightly touched and a toothpick inserted in center comes out clean. Cool layer cakes in pans on wire racks for 10 minutes. Remove cakes from pans. Cool thoroughly on racks. Or, place 13×9-inch cake in pan on a wire rack; cool thoroughly. Frost with Chocolate-Sour Cream Frosting. Cover and store in refrigerator. Makes 16 servings.

Chocolate-Sour Cream Frosting: In saucepan melt one 6-ounce package (1 cup) semisweet chocolate pieces and ¼ cup butter or margarine over low heat, stirring frequently. Cool about 5 minutes. Stir in ½ cup dairy sour cream. Gradually add 2½ cups sifted powdered sugar, beating until smooth and easy to spread.

Nutrition facts per serving: 377 calories, **19 g** total fat (**7 g** saturated fat), **41 mg** cholesterol, **158 mg** sodium, **53 g** carbohydrate, **0 g** fiber, **4 g** protein

 **German Chocolate Cake**
Prep: 50 minutes
Bake: 30 minutes
Cool: 2 hours

1½ cups all-purpose flour
¾ teaspoon baking soda
1 4-ounce package sweet baking chocolate
¾ cup shortening
1 cup sugar
3 eggs
1 teaspoon vanilla
¾ cup buttermilk or sour milk*
1 recipe Coconut-Pecan Frosting (see below)
1 recipe Chocolate Butter Frosting (see page 68) (optional)

Grease and lightly flour two 8×1½-inch or 9×1½-inch round baking pans. Mix flour, soda, and ¼ teaspoon salt. Set aside.

In a saucepan combine chocolate and ½ cup water. Cook and stir over low heat until melted; cool.

In a large mixing bowl beat shortening with an electric mixer on medium to high speed for 30 seconds. Add sugar; beat until fluffy. Add eggs and vanilla; beat on low speed until combined; beat on medium speed 1 minute. Stir in chocolate mixture. Add flour mixture and buttermilk alternately to beaten mixture; beat on low speed after each addition until combined. Pour batter into the prepared pans.

Bake in a 350° oven for 30 to 40 minutes or until a toothpick comes out clean. Cool cakes in pans on wire racks for 10 minutes. Remove from pans. Cool thoroughly on wire racks. Spread Coconut-Pecan Frosting over tops of layers; stack layers. If desired, frost the side with Chocolate Butter Frosting. Cover and store in refrigerator. Makes 12 servings.

Coconut-Pecan Frosting: In a medium saucepan slightly beat 1 egg. Stir in one 5-ounce can (⅔ cup) evaporated milk, ⅔ cup sugar, and ¼ cup butter or margarine. Cook and stir over medium heat about 12 minutes or until thickened and bubbly. Remove from heat; stir in 1⅓ cups flaked coconut and ½ cup chopped pecans. Cover and cool thoroughly.

Note: To make sour milk, place 2 teaspoons lemon juice in a 1-cup glass measuring cup. Add enough milk to make ¾ cup total liquid; stir. Let stand for 5 minutes before using.

Nutrition facts per serving (with Coconut-Pecan Frosting): 470 calories, **29 g** total fat (**11 g** saturated fat), **85 mg** cholesterol, **214 mg** sodium, **51 g** carbohydrate, **2 g** fiber, **6 g** protein

In the late 1950s, using a rich coconut-and-nut puddinglike mixture to fill and frost a chocolate cake became popular. Both Sweet Chocolate Layer Cake and Coconut Frosting and Filling earned places in our 1962 cookbook revision, and this pair has appeared in every edition since.

Too bad this kind of dessert isn't made much anymore—many people are missing out! This jelly roll has a deliciously nutty layer of cake spiraling around lots of light and airy whipped cream. It'll make anyone who sees it immediately proclaim: "Whatever that is, I want some!"

Walnut Cream Roll

Prep: 25 minutes   Bake: 12 minutes   Chill: Up to 2 hours

4 egg yolks	½ cup finely chopped
4 egg whites	walnuts
1 teaspoon vanilla	Powdered sugar
½ teaspoon salt	1 cup whipping cream
½ cup granulated sugar	2 tablespoons granulated
¼ cup all-purpose flour	sugar

Grease and flour a 15×10×1-inch baking pan; set aside. In a medium bowl beat egg yolks with electric mixer on high speed about 4 minutes or until thick and lemon-colored. Wash beaters thoroughly. In large bowl combine egg whites, vanilla, and salt. Beat on high speed until soft peaks form (tips curl); gradually add the ½ cup sugar, beating until stiff peaks form (tips stand straight). Fold yolks into whites; carefully fold in flour and nuts. Spread in prepared pan. Bake in 375° oven for 12 minutes or until top springs back when lightly touched.

Immediately loosen edges of cake from pan and turn out onto towel sprinkled with powdered sugar. Starting at short side, roll up cake and towel together. Cool on a wire rack.

Meanwhile, beat cream and the 2 tablespoons sugar with an electric mixer on medium speed until soft peaks form. Unroll cake; remove towel. Spread whipped cream over cake to within 1 inch of edges. Roll up. Cover; chill up to 2 hours. Serves 10.

Nutrition facts per serving: 214 calories, **15 g** total fat (**6 g** saturated fat), **118 mg** cholesterol, **141 mg** sodium, **17 g** carbohydrate, **0 g** fiber, **4 g** protein

Be sure to use real butter for this frosting. It is essential to obtain a creamy texture and rich flavor—margarine or another spread isn't a satisfactory substitute.

Chocolate Butter Frosting

Start to finish: 20 minutes

⅓ cup butter	¼ cup milk
4 cups sifted powdered	1½ teaspoons vanilla
sugar	Milk (optional)
½ cup unsweetened cocoa	
powder	

Beat butter until fluffy. Gradually add 2 cups of the powdered sugar and the cocoa powder, beating well. Slowly beat in the ¼ cup milk and the vanilla. Gradually add remaining powdered sugar, beating until combined. If necessary, beat in a little additional milk to make frosting that is easy to spread. Makes enough to frost tops and sides of two 8- or 9-inch cake layers, top of one 13×9-inch cake, or 24 cupcakes.

Nutrition facts per serving (¹⁄₁₂ of recipe): 192 calories, **6 g** total fat (**3 g** saturated fat), **14 mg** cholesterol, **54 mg** sodium, **35 g** carbohydrate, **0 g** fiber, **1 g** protein

1953

Peanut Butter Cupcakes

Prep: 15 minutes   Bake: 20 minutes   Cool: 1 hour

½ **cup peanut butter**	2 **cups all-purpose flour**
⅓ **cup shortening**	2 **teaspoons baking**
1 **teaspoon vanilla**	**powder**
1½ **cups packed brown**	½ **teaspoon salt**
sugar	¾ **cup milk**
2 **eggs**	

Line twenty-four 2½-inch muffin cups with paper bake cups; set aside. In a large bowl beat the peanut butter, shortening, and vanilla with electric mixer on medium to high speed for 30 seconds. Gradually add brown sugar, beating until light and fluffy. Add eggs, 1 at a time, beating well after each. Combine flour, baking powder, and salt. Add flour mixture and milk alternately to peanut butter mixture. Fill bake cups half full.

Bake in a 375° oven about 20 minutes or until a toothpick inserted in centers comes out clean. Cool. Makes about 24.

Nutrition facts per cupcake: 145 calories, **6 g** total fat (**1 g** saturated fat), **18 mg** cholesterol, **113 mg** sodium, **20 g** carbohydrate, **1 g** fiber, **3 g** protein

Kids loved peanut butter in the 1950s as much as they love it today. These kid-pleasing cupcakes are fun for everyone, partly because you'll never run out of tasty topping ideas. Chocolate frosting is always a runaway hit, but we also like spreading a little peanut butter on top or dusting them with powdered sugar.

 1946

Black Cherry Dessert Cake

Prep: 20 minutes   Bake: 25 minutes   Cool: 30 minutes

3 **eggs**	1⅓ **cups pitted dark sweet**
1 **cup sugar**	**cherries or one**
½ **teaspoon vanilla**	**16½-ounce can pitted**
¼ **teaspoon almond**	**dark sweet cherries,**
extract	**well drained**
1¾ **cups all-purpose flour**	¼ **cup chopped walnuts**
2 **teaspoons baking**	**Sweetened whipped**
powder	**cream (optional)**

Grease and lightly flour two 8×1½-inch or 9×1½-inch round baking pans; set aside. In large bowl beat eggs with an electric mixer on medium to high speed until light. Gradually add sugar, beating until slightly thickened and lemon colored. Beat in vanilla, almond extract, and 2 tablespoons water. Beat in the flour, baking powder, and ⅛ teaspoon salt just until combined. Spread evenly in prepared baking pans. Sprinkle with cherries and nuts. Bake in 350° oven for 25 to 30 minutes or until toothpick inserted near the center comes out clean. Cool on wire racks for 10 minutes. Remove from pans. Serve slightly warm. If desired, top with sweetened whipped cream. Serves 10 to 12.

Nutrition facts per serving: 204 calories, **4 g** total fat (**1 g** saturated fat), **64 mg** cholesterol, **119 mg** sodium, **5 g** carbohydrate, **1 g** fiber, **5 g** protein

When you taste this cake, you'll find it hard to believe there's no butter or shortening in it, but it's true. This cake has both the texture and flavor of the richest shortcakes and creamed butter cakes. If two layers are more than you need, wrap one tightly in plastic freezer wrap and freeze to enjoy later.

A version of Pineapple Upside-Down Cake was in our 1930 cookbook as Pineapple Skillet Sponge. What made this easy dessert so popular then is the same today: the brown sugar, butter, and pineapple juices bake up to form a scrumptious topping for the fruit and cake.

Pineapple Upside-Down Cake

Prep: 20 minutes   Bake: 30 minutes   Cool: 30 minutes

2 tablespoons butter	1⅓ cups all-purpose flour
⅓ cup packed brown sugar	⅔ cup granulated sugar
1 tablespoon water	2 teaspoons baking powder
1 8-ounce can pineapple slices, drained and halved	⅔ cup milk
	¼ cup butter, softened
4 maraschino cherries, halved	1 egg
	1 teaspoon vanilla

Melt the 2 tablespoons butter in a 9×1½-inch round baking pan.* Stir in brown sugar and water. Arrange pineapple and cherries in the pan; set aside.

In a medium mixing bowl stir together flour, granulated sugar, and baking powder. Add milk, the ¼ cup butter, egg, and vanilla. Beat with an electric mixer on low speed until combined. Beat on medium speed for 1 minute. Spoon batter into the prepared pan.

Bake in a 350° oven for 30 to 35 minutes or until a toothpick comes out clean. Cool in pan on a wire rack for 5 minutes. Loosen side; invert onto a plate. Serve warm. Makes 8 servings.

Note: To melt the butter, place it in the baking pan and place in oven while oven preheats.

Nutrition facts per serving: 286 calories, **10 g** total fat (**6 g** saturated fat), **51 mg** cholesterol, **201 mg** sodium, **47 g** carbohydrate, **1 g** fiber, **4 g** protein

Walnut Torte
Prep: 30 minutes   Bake: 30 minutes   Chill: ½ hour to 6 hours

½ **cup sugar**	⅛ **teaspoon cream of tartar**
½ **cup shortening**	1 **cup sugar**
4 **egg yolks**	¾ **cup finely chopped**
½ **teaspoon vanilla**	**walnuts**
1 **cup all-purpose flour**	¾ **cup sugar**
1 **teaspoon baking powder**	⅓ **cup unsweetened cocoa**
Dash salt	**powder**
⅓ **cup milk**	1½ **cups whipping cream**
4 **egg whites**	

Grease and flour two 8×1½-inch or 9×1½-inch round baking pans; set aside. In a medium mixing bowl beat together the ½ cup sugar and shortening with an electric mixer on medium speed until fluffy. Add egg yolks, 1 at a time, beating 1 minute after each addition. Add vanilla. Stir together flour, baking powder, and salt. Add flour mixture and milk alternately to egg yolk mixture, beating on low speed after each addition until combined. Spread evenly into prepared pans; set aside.

Wash beaters thoroughly. For the meringue, in a large mixing bowl beat egg whites and cream of tartar until soft peaks form (tips curl). Gradually add the 1 cup sugar, beating until stiff peaks form (tips stand straight). By hand, fold in walnuts. Spread meringue evenly over batter in pans. Bake in a 350° oven for 30 to 35 minutes or until a toothpick inserted in center comes out clean. Cool in pans on wire racks for 10 minutes. Carefully loosen cakes from pans; invert pans to remove cakes. Turn cakes meringue sides up; cool completely on wire racks.

For chocolate whip, in medium mixing bowl combine the ¾ cup sugar and the cocoa powder. Gradually stir in whipping cream. Beat just until soft peaks form. Place a cake layer on a serving plate, meringue side up. Spread half of the chocolate whip over layer. Top with second cake layer, meringue side up; spread top with remaining chocolate whip. Cover loosely. Chill in the refrigerator for at least 30 minutes or up to 6 hours. Makes 10 to 12 servings.

Nutrition facts per serving: 535 calories, **32 g** total fat (**12 g** saturated fat), **135 mg** cholesterol, **94 mg** sodium, **59 g** carbohydrate, **1 g** fiber, **7 g** protein

Tortes are a little different from ordinary layer cakes in that they usually have more—but thinner—layers, and are quite a bit richer. Our Walnut Torte follows that blueprint for sinful success with four layers—two cake, two meringue—and a wonderfully decadent chocolate whip frosting.

Cream Puff (see
opposite page) with
Chocolate Pudding

 Vanilla Pudding
Prep: 20 minutes
Chill: 4 hours

¾ cup sugar
3 tablespoons cornstarch
   or all-purpose flour
3 cups milk
4 beaten egg yolks or
   2 beaten eggs
1 tablespoon margarine
   or butter
1½ teaspoons vanilla

In our 1930 cookbook, this basic dessert was called Cornstarch Pudding and had twice as much cornstarch, no eggs, and called for "1 teaspoonful of flavoring." By 1937, the cookbook included several flavor variations of Cornstarch Pudding, including chocolate, butterscotch, orange, and caramel.

In a heavy medium saucepan combine sugar and cornstarch or flour. Stir in milk. Cook and stir over medium heat until bubbly. Cook and stir for 2 minutes more. Remove from heat. Gradually stir 1 cup of the hot milk mixture into egg yolks or eggs.

Stir egg mixture into milk mixture in saucepan. If using egg yolks, bring to a gentle boil; if using whole eggs, cook until nearly bubbly but do not boil. Reduce heat. Cook and stir for 2 minutes more. Remove from heat. Stir in margarine or butter and vanilla. Pour pudding into a bowl; cover with plastic wrap. Chill in refrigerator about 4 hours or until thoroughly chilled. (Do not stir during chilling.) Makes 6 servings.

Chocolate Pudding: Prepare as above, except add ⅓ cup unsweetened cocoa powder along with the sugar. Use 2 tablespoons cornstarch or ¼ cup all-purpose flour, 2⅔ cups milk, and 4 egg yolks (not whole eggs).

Nutrition facts per serving: 232 calories, **8 g** total fat (**3 g** saturated fat), **151 mg** cholesterol, **89 mg** sodium, **35 g** carbohydrate, **0 g** fiber, **6 g** protein
    Nutrition facts per serving Chocolate Pudding: 251 calories, **8 g** total fat (**3 g** saturated fat)

1937 Cream Puffs
Prep: 30 minutes   Bake: 30 minutes

1 **cup water**	**Chocolate or vanilla**
½ **cup butter**	**pudding, sweetened**
⅛ **teaspoon salt**	**whipped cream, or ice**
1 **cup all-purpose flour**	**cream**
4 **eggs**	**Powdered sugar**
	(optional)

In a medium saucepan combine water, butter, and salt. Bring to boiling. Add flour all at once, stirring vigorously. Cook and stir until mixture forms a ball. Remove from heat. Cool for 10 minutes. Add eggs, 1 at a time, beating well with a wooden spoon after each addition.

Grease baking sheet. Drop dough by 12 heaping tablespoons onto prepared baking sheet. Bake in a 400° oven for 30 to 35 minutes or until golden brown. Transfer cream puffs to wire rack; cool completely.

Cut tops from puffs; remove soft dough from insides. Fill with pudding, whipped cream, or ice cream. Replace tops. If desired, sift powdered sugar over tops. Makes 12 cream puffs.

Éclairs: Prepare as above, except spoon dough into a decorating bag fitted with a large plain round tip (about ½-inch opening). Pipe 12 strips of dough, 3 inches apart, onto a greased baking sheet, making each strip 4 inches long, 1 inch wide, and ¾ inch high. Bake, split, and cool as above. Fill éclairs with whipped cream or pudding. For glaze, in small saucepan melt 4 ounces semisweet chocolate, cut up, and 3 tablespoons butter over low heat, stirring frequently. Remove from heat. Stir in 1½ cups sifted powdered sugar and 3 tablespoons hot water. If needed, stir in additional hot water to reach drizzling consistency. Spoon over éclairs. Makes 12 éclairs.

Nutrition facts per puff with ¼ cup chocolate pudding: 207 calories, **11 g** total fat (**6 g** saturated fat), **99 mg** cholesterol, **205 mg** sodium, **22 g** carbohydrate, **0 g** fiber, **5 g** protein

Nutrition facts per éclair with ¼ cup whipped cream and glaze: 347 calories, **26 g** total fat (**16 g** saturated fat), **140 mg** cholesterol, **162 mg** sodium, **27 g** carbohydrate, **1 g** fiber, **4 g** protein

Our cream puff recipe of yesteryear was virtually the same as today's with one important exception— it was made with shortening instead of butter.

When you pull a treasured cookbook off your shelf and flip through the pages, it's easy to see which recipes are favorites. Splatters, crinkled paper, notes written in the margins—they're all telltale signs of a family favorite. So be advised: Cheese-Marbled Brownies has been one of our favorites for a long time—count on this page getting lots of use over the years.

 Cheese-Marbled Brownies

Prep: 20 minutes   Bake: 40 minutes

1 cup semisweet chocolate pieces (6 ounces)	½ cup all-purpose flour
	½ teaspoon baking powder
6 tablespoons margarine or butter	1 8-ounce package cream cheese, softened
⅓ cup honey	½ cup sugar
3 eggs	Dash salt
1 teaspoon vanilla	½ cup chopped walnuts

Grease a 9×9×2-inch baking pan; set aside. In a medium saucepan melt chocolate pieces and margarine or butter over low heat, stirring constantly. Cool slightly. Stir in honey, 2 of the eggs, and the vanilla until combined. Add flour and baking powder, stirring just until flour is moistened. Pour half of the batter into prepared pan. Bake in a 350° oven for 10 minutes.

Meanwhile, in mixing bowl beat together cream cheese and sugar. Beat in remaining egg and the salt. Stir in nuts. Pour mixture over partially baked layer. Spoon remaining chocolate batter over filling. Using a knife, cut through batters to marble. Bake for 30 to 35 minutes more or until a toothpick inserted near center comes out clean. Cool; cut into bars. Makes 24 brownies.

Nutrition facts per brownie: 157 calories, **10 g** total fat (**3 g** saturated fat), **38 mg** cholesterol, **79 mg** sodium, **15 g** carbohydrate, **0 g** fiber, **2 g** protein

These chewy bars were simply called Brownies in 1930, but today we add the descriptor "fudge" to distinguish them from their more cakelike cousins. Double the delight by topping the cooled brownies with your favorite chocolate frosting.

1930 Fudge Brownies

Prep: 15 minutes   Bake: 30 minutes

½ cup butter	1 cup sugar
2 ounces unsweetened chocolate	1 teaspoon vanilla
	¾ cup all-purpose flour
2 eggs	½ cup chopped nuts

Grease an 8×8×2-inch baking pan; set aside. In a medium saucepan melt butter and chocolate over low heat. Remove from heat. Stir in eggs, sugar, and vanilla. Using a wooden spoon, beat lightly until just combined. Stir in flour and nuts.

Spread in prepared pan. Bake in a 350° oven for 30 minutes. Cool in pan on a wire rack. Cut into bars. Makes 24 brownies.

Nutrition facts per brownie: 113 calories, **7 g** total fat (**3 g** saturated fat), **28 mg** cholesterol, **44 mg** sodium, **12 g** carbohydrate, **0 g** fiber, **2 g** protein

Date Layer Bars
Prep: 20 minutes   Bake: 35 minutes

½ **cup butter**	1 **tablespoon water**
1 **cup packed brown**	1¾ **cups chopped pitted**
sugar	**dates (about**
1½ **cups all-purpose flour**	**10 ounces)**
½ **teaspoon baking soda**	1½ **cups water**
½ **teaspoon salt**	½ **cup raisins**
1 **cup quick-cooking**	
rolled oats	

In a large mixing bowl beat the butter with an electric mixer on medium to high speed for 30 seconds. Add the brown sugar; beat until combined. Beat in the flour, baking soda, and salt until crumbly. Stir in the oats and the 1 tablespoon water until combined. Press half of the rolled oats mixture into the bottom of 13×9×2-inch baking pan.

For filling, in a medium saucepan combine dates, 1½ cups water, and raisins. Bring to boiling; reduce heat. Cover and simmer for 8 to 10 minutes or until thickened.

Spread filling evenly over rolled oats mixture in pan. Sprinkle filling evenly with remaining rolled oats mixture, pressing slightly into filling.

Bake in a 350° oven about 35 minutes or until golden. Cool in pan on a wire rack. Cut into bars. Makes 32 bars.

Nutrition facts per bar: 109 calories, **3 g** total fat (**2 g** saturated fat), **8 mg** cholesterol, **85 mg** sodium, **20 g** carbohydrate, **1 g** fiber, **1 g** protein

The next time you need to take a treat to an event, consider these as a scrumptious alternative to the usual chocolate option. The date-and-raisin filling coupled with a buttery oat topping make these bar cookies an ultimate favorite.

1981 ## Chocolate Revel Bars

Prep: 30 minutes   Bake: 25 minutes

1	cup butter	1½	cups semisweet chocolate pieces
2	cups packed brown sugar	1	14-ounce can (1¼ cups) sweetened condensed milk or low-fat sweetened condensed milk
1	teaspoon baking soda		
2	eggs		
2	teaspoons vanilla		
2½	cups all-purpose flour	½	cup chopped walnuts or pecans
3	cups quick-cooking rolled oats	2	teaspoons vanilla

Set aside 2 tablespoons of the butter. In a large mixing bowl beat the remaining butter with an electric mixer on medium to high speed for 30 seconds. Add the brown sugar and baking soda. Beat until combined, scraping side of bowl occasionally. Beat in eggs and 2 teaspoons vanilla until combined. Beat in as much of the flour as you can with the mixer. Stir in remaining flour. Stir in the rolled oats; set aside.

For filling, in a medium saucepan combine the reserved butter, chocolate pieces, and sweetened condensed milk. Cook over low heat until chocolate melts, stirring occasionally. Remove from heat. Stir in the walnuts or pecans and 2 teaspoons vanilla.

Press two-thirds (about 3⅓ cups) of the rolled oats mixture into the bottom of an ungreased 15×10×1-inch baking pan. Spread filling evenly over the oat mixture. Dot remaining rolled oats mixture on filling.

Bake in a 350° oven about 25 minutes or until top is lightly browned (chocolate filling will still look moist). Cool in pan on a wire rack. Cut into bars. Makes 60 bars.

Peanut Butter-Chocolate Revel Bars: Prepare as above, except substitute ½ cup peanut butter for the 2 tablespoons butter when making the chocolate filling and substitute peanuts for the walnuts or pecans.

Whole Wheat-Chocolate Revel Bars: Prepare as above, except reduce the all-purpose flour to 1½ cups and add 1 cup whole wheat flour.

Nutrition facts per bar: 148 calories, **6 g** total fat (**2 g** saturated fat), **17 mg** cholesterol, **79 mg** sodium, **21 g** carbohydrate, **1 g** fiber, **3 g** protein
   Nutrition facts per Peanut Butter-Chocolate Revel Bar: 143 calories, **7 g** total fat (**2 g** saturated fat)
   Nutrition facts per Whole Wheat-Chocolate Revel Bar: 133 calories, **6 g** total fat (**2 g** saturated fat)

 Chocolate Chip Cookies

Prep: 25 minutes
Bake: 8 minutes
per cookie sheet

½   cup shortening
½   cup butter
1   cup packed brown
      sugar
½   cup granulated sugar
½   teaspoon baking soda
2   eggs
1   teaspoon vanilla
2½ cups all-purpose flour
1   12-ounce package
      (2 cups) semisweet
      chocolate pieces
1½ cups chopped walnuts,
      pecans, or hazelnuts
      (filberts) (optional)

In a large mixing bowl beat the shortening and butter with an electric mixer on medium to high speed for 30 seconds. Add the brown sugar, granulated sugar, and baking soda. Beat mixture until combined, scraping side of bowl occasionally. Beat in the eggs and vanilla until combined. Beat in as much of the flour as you can with the mixer. Stir in remaining flour. Stir in chocolate pieces and, if desired, nuts.

Drop dough by rounded teaspoons 2 inches apart on an ungreased cookie sheet. Bake in a 375° oven 8 to 10 minutes or until edges are lightly browned. Transfer cookies to a wire rack; cool completely. Makes about 60 cookies.

Macadamia Nut and White Chocolate Chunk Cookies:
Prepare as above, except substitute chopped white baking bars or white chocolate baking squares for the semisweet chocolate pieces. Stir in one 3½-ounce jar macadamia nuts, chopped, with the white chocolate.

Nutrition facts per cookie: 93 calories, **5 g** total fat (**1 g** saturated fat), **11 mg** cholesterol, **29 mg** sodium, **12 g** carbohydrate, **0 g** fiber, **1 g** protein
   Nutrition facts per Macadamia Nut and White Chocolate Chunk Cookie: 108 calories, **6 g** total fat (**3 g** saturated fat)

Old gems, such as this recipe that dates back to our 1941 edition, only get better with age. Try the traditional chocolate chip version and the trendy new macadamia variation— each one is sure to satisfy both your nostalgic and sophisticated sides.

Here's a great recipe we streamlined for today's hectic schedules. Our 1946 recipe was a refrigerator cookie that required forming the dough into rolls, chilling the rolls, then slicing them for baking. We converted the recipe into a quick and easy drop-cookie method that will have you enjoying that fantastic old-fashioned flavor in a fraction of the time.

 ### Oatmeal Crispies
Prep: 20 minutes   Bake: 10 minutes per cookie sheet

1 cup shortening	2 eggs
1 cup granulated sugar	1 teaspoon vanilla
1 cup packed brown sugar	1½ cups all-purpose flour
1 teaspoon baking soda	3 cups quick-cooking rolled oats
½ teaspoon salt	½ cup chopped walnuts

In a large mixing bowl beat shortening with an electric mixer on medium to high speed for 30 seconds. Add the granulated sugar, brown sugar, baking soda, and salt. Beat until combined. Beat in eggs and vanilla until combined. Beat in as much of the flour as you can with the mixer. Stir in any remaining flour, the oats, and walnuts. Drop dough by tablespoons 2 inches apart on an ungreased cookie sheet.

Bake cookies in a 350° oven about 10 minutes or until lightly browned. Transfer cookies to a wire rack; cool completely. Makes about 72 cookies.

Nutrition facts per cookie: 74 calories, **4 g** total fat (**1 g** saturated fat), **6 mg** cholesterol, **35 mg** sodium, **9 g** carbohydrate, **0 g** fiber, **1 g** protein

Here's an example of how tastes can change with the times. In 1946, this raspberry pie debuted with a cornflake crust. We decided to update the pie with a good ol' graham cracker crust. And in the process we rediscovered just how light and refreshing a pie this is—perfect to enjoy outside on an idyllic summer's day.

 ### Raspberry Pie
Prep: 1 hour   Chill: 4 hours to overnight

3 cups fresh red or black raspberries	1 tablespoon lemon juice
½ cup sugar	1 9-inch graham cracker crust*
1 envelope unflavored gelatin	1 cup whipping cream
¾ cup cold water	2 tablespoons sugar

In large saucepan slightly crush berries. Add the ½ cup sugar. Let stand for 10 minutes. Meanwhile, soften gelatin in cold water about 5 minutes. Add gelatin mixture to saucepan. Heat and stir until gelatin is dissolved. Stir in lemon juice; cool. Cover and chill until partially set (consistency of unbeaten egg whites). Pour chilled mixture into crust. Cover and chill in refrigerator at least 4 hours or overnight or until set.

Just before serving, in a mixing bowl combine whipping cream and the 2 tablespoons sugar. Whip until soft peaks form. Spread over entire pie. Makes 8 servings.

***Note:** If you purchase a crust, be sure to buy a 9-ounce one so that the crust is large enough to hold all of the filling.

Nutrition facts per serving: 189 calories, **11 g** total fat (**7 g** saturated fat), **41 mg** cholesterol, **13 mg** sodium, **22 g** carbohydrate, **2 g** fiber, **2 g** protein

1930 **Pastry for Single-Crust Pie**
Prep: 10 minutes

1¼ cups all-purpose flour	4 to 5 tablespoons cold water
¼ teaspoon salt	
⅓ cup shortening	

Stir together flour and salt. Using a pastry blender, cut in shortening until pieces are pea-size.

Sprinkle 1 tablespoon of the water over part of the mixture; gently toss with a fork. Push moistened dough to side of bowl. Repeat, using 1 tablespoon water at a time, until all the dough is moistened. Form dough into a ball. On lightly floured surface, flatten dough. Roll from center to edge into a circle about 12 inches in diameter.

To transfer pastry, wrap it around the rolling pin; unroll into a 9-inch pie plate. Ease pastry into pie plate, being careful not to stretch pastry.

Trim pastry to ½ inch beyond edge of pie plate. Fold under extra pastry. Crimp edge as desired. Do not prick pastry. Bake as directed in individual recipes. Makes 8 servings.

Pastry for Double-Crust Pie: Prepare pastry dough as above, except use 2 cups all-purpose flour, ½ teaspoon salt, ⅔ cup shortening, and 6 to 7 tablespoons cold water. Divide dough in half. Form each half into a ball. Roll 1 dough ball as above; transfer to pie plate as above. Transfer filling to pastry-lined pie plate. Trim pastry even with rim of pie plate.

Roll remaining dough into a circle about 12 inches in diameter. Cut slits to allow steam to escape. Place remaining pastry on filling; trim ½ inch beyond edge of plate. Fold top pastry under bottom pastry. Crimp edge as desired. Bake as directed in individual recipes. Makes 8 servings.

Nutrition facts per serving: 141 calories, **9 g** total fat (**2 g** saturated fat), **0 mg** cholesterol, **67 mg** sodium, **14 g** carbohydrate, **0 g** fiber, **2 g** protein
    Nutrition facts per serving Pastry for Double-Crust Pie: 256 calories, **17 g** total fat (**4 g** saturated fat), **0 mg** cholesterol, **134 mg** sodium, **22 g** carbohydrate, **1 g** fiber, **3 g** protein

There was a time when home cooks were judged by their ability to make light, flaky pastry. This recipe, originally appearing in the 1930s, has helped generations of cooks pass the pastry test.

*Pumpkin pie aficionados
are a patient lot.
Only one day a year
celebrates their dessert
passion. Then, another
entire year passes
before pumpkin pie
miraculously reappears.
This extraordinary
pie, adorned with a
caramelized brown
sugar and pecan
topping, is worth
waiting for all year—
but there's no reason
why you should.*

 Caramel Pecan Pumpkin Pie
Prep: 15 minutes   Bake: 45 minutes

1 recipe Pastry for Single-Crust Pie (see page 79)	¼ teaspoon salt
2 slightly beaten eggs	¼ teaspoon ground cinnamon
1 15-ounce can pumpkin	¼ teaspoon ground nutmeg
¼ cup half-and-half or milk	⅛ teaspoon ground allspice
¾ cup granulated sugar	½ cup packed brown sugar
1 tablespoon all-purpose flour	½ cup chopped pecans
1 teaspoon finely shredded lemon peel	2 tablespoons butter, softened
½ teaspoon vanilla	

Prepare pastry and line pie plate as directed. In a large bowl
stir together eggs, pumpkin, and half-and-half or milk. Stir in
the granulated sugar, flour, lemon peel, vanilla, salt,
cinnamon, nutmeg, and allspice. Pour pumpkin mixture into
pastry-lined pie plate. To prevent overbrowning, cover the edge
of the pie with foil. Bake in a 375° oven for 25 minutes.

Meanwhile, in a medium bowl stir together the brown sugar,
pecans, and butter until combined. Remove foil. Sprinkle brown
sugar mixture over top of pie. Bake for 20 minutes more or until
a knife inserted near the center comes out clean and topping is
golden and bubbly. Cool on a wire rack. Cover and refrigerate
within 2 hours. Makes 8 servings.

Nutrition facts per serving: 377 calories, **18 g** total fat (**5 g** saturated fat),
63 mg cholesterol, **188 mg** sodium, **50 g** carbohydrate, **3 g** fiber, **5 g** protein

Cranberry-Raisin Crisscross Pie
Prep: 45 minutes   Bake: 50 minutes

¾ **cup raisins**
1¼ **cups sugar**
1 **tablespoon cornstarch**
3 **cups fresh cranberries**
½ **cup orange juice**

1 **recipe Pastry for Double-Crust Pie (see page 79)**
½ **cup chopped walnuts**

Cover raisins with boiling water. Let stand 5 minutes; drain. Stir together sugar and cornstarch. Stir in raisins, cranberries, and juice. Cook and stir over medium heat until bubbly; set aside.

Meanwhile, prepare pastry and line pie plate as directed. Transfer cranberry mixture to pastry-lined pie plate. Sprinkle with nuts. Trim pastry to ½ inch beyond edge of pie plate. Cut remaining pastry into ½-inch-wide strips. Weave strips over filling for lattice crust. Press ends of strips into crust rim. Fold bottom pastry edge over strips; seal and crimp edge. Cover edge with foil. Bake in 375° oven for 25 minutes. Remove foil. Bake 25 minutes more or until golden. Cool on rack. Serves 8.

Nutrition facts per serving: 497 calories, **22 g** total fat (**5 g** saturated fat), **0 mg** cholesterol, **137 mg** sodium, **73 g** carbohydrate, **3 g** fiber, **5 g** protein

One look at a lattice-topped pie tells you that it was made by someone who didn't mind spending an extra 5 to 10 minutes just to delight the eye. This pie combines that warm and inviting look with a clever mix of flavors—cranberry, orange juice, raisin, and walnut—for a can't-miss hit.

Red Raspberry-Cherry Pie
Prep: 25 minutes   Stand: 15 minutes   Bake: 45 minutes

1 **cup sugar**
3 **tablespoons quick-cooking tapioca**
3 **cups fresh or frozen unsweetened pitted tart red cherries**
1½ **cups fresh or frozen lightly sweetened raspberries**

1 **teaspoon lemon juice**
1 **recipe Pastry for Double-Crust Pie (see page 79)**
1 **tablespoon margarine or butter, cut up**

Stir together sugar and tapioca. Add fruits and juice; toss to coat. Let stand 15 minutes (1 hour for frozen fruit) or until syrup forms. Meanwhile, prepare pastry and line pie plate as directed. Transfer berry mixture to pastry-lined pie plate. Trim pastry even with rim of pie plate. Dot with margarine. Place top crust on filling. Seal and crimp. To prevent overbrowning, cover edge with foil. Bake in 375° oven 25 minutes (50 minutes for frozen fruit). Remove foil. Bake 20 to 25 minutes more (20 to 30 minutes more for frozen fruit) or until golden. Cool. Serves 8.

Nutrition facts per serving: 418 calories, **19 g** total fat (**4 g** saturated fat), **0 mg** cholesterol, **151 mg** sodium, **60 g** carbohydrate, **3 g** fiber, **4 g** protein

There are several ingredients you can use to thicken a fruit pie. But one you don't see very often anymore is tapioca. We found that for the nicely balanced, sweet-tart flavor of this pie, nothing works better. Tapioca doesn't mask the great flavor of the berries and cherries, and it thickens into a beautifully clear filling that slices quite nicely.

Apple Pie

1930 Prep: 30 minutes   Bake: 50 minutes

1 recipe Pastry for Double-Crust Pie (see page 79)	¾ cup sugar
	2 tablespoons all-purpose flour
6 cups thinly sliced, peeled cooking apples* (about 2¼ pounds)	½ teaspoon ground cinnamon
	⅛ teaspoon ground nutmeg
1 tablespoon lemon juice (optional)	½ cup raisins or chopped walnuts (optional)

Prepare pastry and line pie plate as directed. If desired, sprinkle apples with lemon juice. In a large mixing bowl stir together sugar, flour, cinnamon, and nutmeg. Add apple slices and, if desired, raisins or walnuts. Gently toss to coat.

Transfer apple mixture to the pastry-lined pie plate. Trim pastry to edge of pie plate. Place top crust on filling. Seal and crimp.

To prevent overbrowning, cover edge of pie with foil. Bake in a 375° oven for 25 minutes. Remove foil. Bake for 25 to 30 minutes more or until top is golden. Cool on wire rack. Makes 8 servings.

***Note:** Good apple choices include Cortland, Golden Delicious, Granny Smith, Newtown Pippin, Rome Beauty, Stayman, Winesap, and York Imperial.

Nutrition facts per serving: 380 calories, **18 g** total fat (**4 g** saturated fat), **0 mg** cholesterol, **135 mg** sodium, **54 g** carbohydrate, **3 g** fiber, **3 g** protein

Deep-Dish Strawberry-Rhubarb Pie

Prep: 30 minutes   Bake: 50 minutes

¾ to 1 cup sugar	1 tablespoon butter or
¼ cup cornstarch	margarine, cut up
3 cups fresh or frozen	1 recipe Pastry for
strawberries, halved	Single-Crust Pie
3 cups fresh or frozen	(see page 79)
rhubarb	Sugar

Combine ¾ to 1 cup sugar, cornstarch, and ⅛ teaspoon salt. Add fruits. Gently toss to coat. (If using frozen fruit, let stand 15 to 30 minutes or until fruit is partially thawed, but still icy.) Transfer to a 9-inch deep-dish pie plate. Dot with butter. Prepare pastry dough as directed. On lightly floured surface, roll pastry dough into a 12-inch circle. Cut slits. Place pastry on filling. Seal and crimp to the rim of the pie plate. Sprinkle with sugar. Place on a baking sheet. Cover edge of pie with foil. Bake in a 375° oven for 25 minutes (50 minutes for frozen fruit). Remove foil. Bake for 25 to 30 minutes more (about 30 minutes more for frozen fruit) or until top is golden. Cool on rack. Serves 8.

Nutrition facts per serving: 292 calories, **10 g** total fat (**3 g** saturated fat), **4 mg** cholesterol, **118 mg** sodium, **43 g** carbohydrate, **2 g** fiber, **3 g** protein

In the 1930s pies were usually much, much thinner than they are today. So for the times, this deep-dish pie was a monster. Why did they make it so big? For one thing, strawberries and rhubarb were plentiful in many backyard gardens every spring. But perhaps an even bigger factor was at work: For many, strawberry-rhubarb is the one pie that can't be too big!

Raisin Cream Pie

Prep: 20 minutes   Bake: 30 minutes

1 recipe Pastry for	½ teaspoon ground
Single-Crust Pie (see	cinnamon
page 79)	½ teaspoon ground
3 slightly beaten eggs	nutmeg
1 cup sugar	¼ teaspoon salt
2 tablespoons lemon juice	1 cup raisins
2 tablespoons margarine	½ cup chopped walnuts
or butter, melted	

Prepare pastry and line pie plate as directed. Stir together eggs, sugar, lemon juice, margarine, cinnamon, nutmeg, and salt. Add raisins and walnuts; mix until just combined. Pour raisin-nut mixture into the pastry-lined pie plate. Bake in a 375° oven for 30 minutes or until center is set. Cool on a wire rack. Cover and refrigerate within 2 hours. Makes 8 servings.

Nutrition facts per serving: 396 calories, **18 g** total fat (**4 g** saturated fat), **80 mg** cholesterol, **190 mg** sodium, **55 g** carbohydrate, **2 g** fiber, **6 g** protein

Can cream pie have no cream? Well, we confess that this pie isn't exactly your ordinary cream pie like, say, a banana cream pie. It's something all its own. The flavor and texture is a little like pecan pie, but the addition of sweet, plump, juicy raisins adds an entirely different and deliciously indescribable dimension. So until we can come up with a better name, Raisin Cream Pie it must remain.

When cheesecake first ran in a 1940s' edition of our cookbook as a novelty recipe, who would have believed that it would surpass apple pie as America's favorite dessert.

1941 Cheesecake Supreme
Prep: 40 minutes   Bake: 45 minutes   Chill: At least 4 hours

1¾	cups finely crushed graham crackers	2	tablespoons all-purpose flour
¼	cup finely chopped walnuts	1	teaspoon vanilla
½	teaspoon ground cinnamon	½	teaspoon finely shredded lemon peel (optional)
½	cup butter, melted	2	eggs
3	8-ounce packages cream cheese, softened	1	egg yolk
1	cup sugar	¼	cup milk
			Fresh raspberries (optional)

For crust, combine crushed graham crackers, walnuts, and cinnamon. Stir in melted butter. If desired, reserve ¼ cup of the crumb mixture for topping. Press the remaining crumb mixture onto the bottom and about 2 inches up side of an 8- or 9-inch springform pan. Set pan aside.

For filling, in a large mixing bowl beat cream cheese, sugar, flour, vanilla, and, if desired, lemon peel with an electric mixer until combined. Add eggs and egg yolk all at once, beating on low speed just until combined. Stir in milk.

Pour filling into crust-lined pan. If desired, sprinkle with reserved crumbs. Place on a shallow baking pan in oven. Bake in a 375° oven for 45 to 50 minutes for the 8-inch pan, 35 to 40 minutes for the 9-inch pan, or until center appears nearly set when shaken.

Cool in pan on a wire rack for 15 minutes. Loosen the crust from side of pan; cool 30 minutes more. Remove the side of the pan; cool cheesecake completely. Cover and chill in refrigerator at least 4 hours before serving. If desired, garnish with raspberries. Makes 12 to 16 servings.

Sour Cream Cheesecake: Prepare as above, except reduce cream cheese to 2 packages and omit the milk. Add three 8-ounce cartons dairy sour cream with the eggs. Bake about 55 minutes for 8-inch pan or about 50 minutes for 9-inch pan.

Chocolate Cheesecake: Prepare as above, except omit lemon peel. Melt 4 ounces semisweet chocolate. Beat the melted chocolate into the filling mixture just before adding the eggs.

Chocolate Swirl Cheesecake: Prepare cheesecake as above, except omit lemon peel. Melt 2 ounces semisweet chocolate. Stir the melted chocolate into half of the filling. Pour chocolate filling into the crust; pour plain filling into the crust. Using a spatula, gently swirl fillings.

Low-Fat Cheesecake: Prepare as above, except reduce crushed crackers to ⅓ cup and omit walnuts, cinnamon, and butter. Sprinkle crackers on bottom and side of a well-buttered 8- or 9-inch springform pan. Substitute three 8-ounce packages

fat-free cream cheese for the regular cream cheese and ½ cup refrigerated or frozen egg product (thawed) for the eggs and egg yolk. Bake in a 375° oven for 45 to 50 minutes for the 8-inch pan, 35 to 40 minutes for the 9-inch pan, or until center appears nearly set when shaken. Cool in pan on a wire rack for 15 minutes. Loosen the crust from side of pan; cool 30 minutes more. Remove the side of the pan; cool cheesecake completely. Cover and chill in refrigerator for at least 4 hours before serving. If desired, serve with fresh fruit such as strawberries, raspberries, blueberries, and/or kiwifruit.

Nutrition facts per serving: 429 calories, **32 g** total fat (**18 g** saturated fat), **137 mg** cholesterol, **329 mg** sodium, **30 g** carbohydrate, **1 g** fiber, **7 g** protein
    Nutrition facts per serving Sour Cream Cheesecake: 481 calories, **37 g** total fat (**21 g** saturated fat)
    Nutrition facts per serving Chocolate Cheesecake: 477 calories, **35 g** total fat (**20 g** saturated fat)
    Nutrition facts per serving Chocolate Swirl Cheesecake: 451 calories, **33 g** total fat (**19 g** saturated fat)
    Nutrition facts per serving Low-Fat Cheesecake: 141 calories, **1 g** total fat (**0 g** saturated fat), **10 mg** cholesterol

 Concord Grape Pie

Prep: 30 minutes
Bake: 45 minutes

1	recipe Pastry for Single-Crust Pie (see page 79)
1½	pounds Concord grapes (4 cups)
¾	cup sugar
⅓	cup all-purpose flour
¼	teaspoon salt
2	tablespoons butter, melted
1	tablespoon lemon juice
½	cup all-purpose flour
½	cup sugar
¼	cup butter

Concord grapes are available only in late summer and early fall, but they're well worth the wait—especially for making a pie. Concords are "slip-skin" grapes, which means that their skins pop right off with a gentle squeeze. But even more importantly, their special flavor is deep and dark, the perfect balance of sweet and tart.

Prepare pastry and line pie plate as directed; set aside. Remove skins from grapes by gently pressing each grape between your fingers. The skins will slip off easily. Set skins aside. In a large saucepan bring grape pulp to boiling; reduce heat. Simmer, uncovered, for 5 minutes. Sieve the pulp to remove the seeds. Add the grape skins to the pulp.

In a large mixing bowl stir together the ¾ cup sugar, the ⅓ cup flour, and the salt. Stir in the grape mixture, melted butter, and lemon juice. Pour mixture into the pastry-lined pie plate. To prevent overbrowning, cover the edge of the pie with foil. Bake in a 375° oven for 20 minutes.

Meanwhile, stir together the ½ cup flour and the ½ cup sugar. Cut in the ¼ cup butter until mixture resembles coarse crumbs. Remove foil from pie. Sprinkle crumb mixture over pie. Bake about 25 minutes more or until topping is golden brown. Cool on a wire rack. Makes 8 servings.

Nutrition facts per serving: 402 calories, **18 g** total fat (**4 g** saturated fat), **23 mg** cholesterol, **223 mg** sodium, **61 g** carbohydrate, **2 g** fiber, **4 g** protein

Lemon Sponge Pie
Prep: 25 minutes   Bake: 30 minutes

1 recipe Pastry for Single-Crust Pie (see page 79)	3 slightly beaten egg yolks
1 cup sugar	2 teaspoons finely shredded lemon peel
3 tablespoons all-purpose flour	3 tablespoons lemon juice
¼ cup butter or margarine, melted	2 cups milk
	3 egg whites

Prepare pastry and line pie plate as directed, crimping edge high. Line pastry with a double thickness of foil. Bake in a 450° oven for 8 minutes. Remove foil; bake 4 to 5 minutes more or until pastry is set and dry. Set aside. Reduce oven temperature to 350°.

For filling, in a medium bowl stir together sugar and flour. Stir in melted butter or margarine. Add egg yolks, lemon peel, and lemon juice. Stir in milk. Set aside. In a medium mixing bowl beat egg whites with an electric mixer on high speed until stiff peaks form (tips stand straight). Fold egg whites into milk mixture.

Place pastry-lined pie plate on oven rack. Carefully pour filling into partially baked pastry shell. Bake in a 350° oven for 30 minutes or until top springs back when lightly touched. Cool on a wire rack. Cover and refrigerate within 2 hours. Makes 8 servings.

Nutrition facts per serving: 358 calories, **18 g** total fat (**7 g** saturated fat), **100 mg** cholesterol, **179 mg** sodium, **45 g** carbohydrate, **1 g** fiber, **7 g** protein

Imagine crossing lemon pie with a lemon cake. The result would be Lemon Sponge Pie. This refreshing dessert consists of a perfect flaky pie crust, a creamy, custardy filling with just the right amount of lemon tartness, and a delicate mantle of the lightest, airiest lemon-flavor cake imaginable. Try it for yourself and see!

The combination of a rich chocolate sauce, a layer of peppermint ice cream, and meringue makes this pie a dream-come-true for anyone craving the ultimate dessert indulgence. And if you're short on time, you can greatly streamline the recipe by replacing the meringue topping with sweetened whipped cream—and omitting the baking. Either way, for an over-the-top dessert experience, you couldn't ask for more.

Fudge Ribbon Pie
Prep: 50 minutes   Bake: 3 minutes   Freeze: Several hours

1	recipe Pastry for Single-Crust Pie (see page 79)
1	cup sugar
1	5-ounce can (⅔ cup) evaporated milk
2	tablespoons butter
2	ounces unsweetened chocolate, cut up
1½	teaspoons vanilla

2	pints (4 cups) peppermint ice cream
2	tablespoons dried egg whites (see note, page 91)
¼	teaspoon cream of tartar
6	tablespoons sugar
¼	cup crushed peppermint-stick candy

Prepare pastry and line pie plate as directed. Generously prick bottom and sides of pastry in pie plate with a fork. Prick all around where bottom and side meet. Line pastry with a double thickness of foil. Bake in a 450° oven for 8 minutes. Remove foil. Bake 5 to 6 minutes more or until golden. Cool on a wire rack.

Meanwhile, for fudge sauce, in a small saucepan combine the 1 cup sugar, the evaporated milk, butter, and chocolate. Cook and stir over medium heat until bubbly. Reduce heat and boil gently for 4 to 5 minutes until mixture is thickened and reduced to 1½ cups, stirring occasionally. Remove from heat; stir in 1 teaspoon of the vanilla. If necessary, beat until smooth with wire whisk or rotary beater. Set aside to cool completely.

In a chilled medium bowl, stir 1 pint of the ice cream until softened. Spread into cooled pastry shell. Cover with half of the cooled fudge sauce. Freeze until nearly firm. Repeat with remaining ice cream and fudge sauce. Return to freezer while preparing meringue.

For meringue, in medium mixing bowl reconstitute dried egg whites according to package directions; stir in remaining vanilla and cream of tartar. Beat with electric mixer on medium speed about 1 minute or until soft peaks form (tips curl). Gradually add the 6 tablespoons sugar, 1 tablespoon at a time, beating on high speed about 4 minutes more or until mixture forms stiff, glossy peaks and sugar dissolves. By hand, fold 3 tablespoons of the crushed candy into the meringue. Spread meringue over chocolate sauce layer, sealing to edge. Sprinkle top with remaining crushed candy. Freeze until firm (several hours or overnight).

Bake in a 475° oven for 3 to 4 minutes or just until meringue is lightly browned. Cover loosely and return to freezer for a few hours or overnight before serving. Makes 8 servings.

Nutrition facts per serving: 537 calories, **24 g** total fat (**11 g** saturated fat), **43 mg** cholesterol, **194 mg** sodium, **77 g** carbohydrate, **1 g** fiber, **6 g** protein

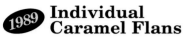

Individual Caramel Flans

Prep: 25 minutes
Bake: 30 minutes

⅓ **cup sugar**
3 **beaten eggs**
1½ **cups milk**
⅓ **cup sugar**
1 **teaspoon vanilla**
   Ground nutmeg or
      cinnamon (optional)

To caramelize sugar, in a heavy 8-inch skillet cook ⅓ cup sugar over medium-high heat until sugar begins to melt, shaking the skillet occasionally to heat the sugar evenly. Do not stir. Once the sugar starts to melt, reduce heat to low. Cook about 5 minutes more or until all of the sugar is melted and golden, stirring as needed with a wooden spoon. Immediately divide the caramelized sugar among four 6-ounce custard cups; tilt custard cups to coat bottoms evenly. Let stand for 10 minutes.

Meanwhile, combine eggs, milk, ⅓ cup sugar, and vanilla. Beat until well combined but not foamy. Place the custard cups in a 2-quart square baking dish on an oven rack. Divide egg mixture among custard cups. If desired, sprinkle with nutmeg or cinnamon. Pour boiling water into the baking dish around custard cups to a depth of 1 inch. Bake in a 325° oven for 30 to 45 minutes or until a knife inserted near the centers comes out clean.

Remove cups from water. Cool slightly on a wire rack before serving. (Or, cool completely in custard cups. Cover and chill in refrigerator until serving time.) To unmold flans, loosen edges with a knife, slipping point down sides to let air in. Invert a dessert plate over each flan; turn custard cup and plate over together. Remove custard cups. Makes 4 servings.

Baked Custards: Prepare as above, except omit the ⅓ cup sugar that is caramelized. Divide egg mixture among custard cups or pour all of egg mixture into one 3½-cup soufflé dish. Bake individual custards as directed above or bake soufflé dish for 50 to 60 minutes. Serve warm or chilled.

Even though Plain Baked Custard was among the desserts in our 1930 cookbook, it wasn't until 1989 that the sophisticated adaptation, flan, appeared. What makes flan extra special is its elegant caramelized sugar topping.

Nutrition facts per serving: 234 calories, **6 g** total fat (**2 g** saturated fat), **167 mg** cholesterol, **94 mg** sodium, **39 g** carbohydrate, **0 g** fiber, **8 g** protein
   Nutrition facts per serving Baked Custards: 170 calories, **6 g** total fat (**2 g** saturated fat)

Cranberry Pudding
Prep: 20 minutes   Steam: 1 hour   Cool: 40 minutes

2 cups all-purpose flour	½ teaspoon finely
4 teaspoons baking powder	shredded orange peel
¼ teaspoon salt	1 orange, peeled,
¾ cup sugar	sectioned, and finely
2 tablespoons shortening	chopped
1 egg	Sweetened whipped
1 cup milk	cream
1 cup chopped fresh	
cranberries	

In a bowl combine the flour, baking powder, and salt; set aside. In a medium mixing bowl beat the sugar and shortening with an electric mixer on medium to high speed until well mixed. Beat in the egg until combined. Add the flour mixture and milk alternately to beaten mixture, beating at low speed just until combined. Gently stir in cranberries, orange peel, and orange.

 Pour into a 7- to 8-cup steamed pudding tube mold. Cover tightly with foil. Place mold on a rack in a deep kettle. Add boiling water to a depth of 1 inch. Cover kettle. Bring to a gentle boil and steam 1 to 1¼ hours or until a long toothpick inserted in center of pudding comes out clean. Add more boiling water to kettle as necessary. Remove mold from kettle. Cool in mold for 10 minutes. Invert mold to remove pudding. Cool on wire rack about 30 minutes. Serve warm with whipped cream. Serves 8.

Nutrition facts per serving: 241 calories, **5 g** total fat (**1 g** saturated fat), **29 mg** cholesterol, **272 mg** sodium, **45 g** carbohydrate, **2 g** fiber, **5 g** protein

Six Threes Ice Cream
Prep: 25 minutes   Freeze: 25 minutes   Ripen: 4 hours

3 cups milk	Juice of 3 oranges (1 cup)
3 cups half-and-half or	3 ripe bananas, mashed
light cream	(1⅓ cups)
3 cups sugar	
Juice of 3 lemons (½ cup)	

Combine milk, half-and-half, and sugar. Stir until sugar dissolves. Add remaining ingredients. Freeze in a 4- or 5-quart ice-cream freezer according to manufacturer's directions. Remove dasher; cover top of can with foil. Plug hole in lid. To ripen, pack outer freezer bucket with enough ice and salt to cover top of can, using 4 cups ice to 1 cup salt; let stand 4 hours. Makes about 3 quarts.

Nutrition facts per ½ cup: 170 calories, **4 g** total fat (**3 g** saturated fat), **13 mg** cholesterol, **28 mg** sodium, **33 g** carbohydrate, **0 g** fiber, **2 g** protein

Black Walnut-Caramel Ice Cream

1946 Prep: 35 minutes   Freeze: 1 hour plus several hours

½ **cup sugar**	4 **teaspoons dried egg**
2 **cups milk**	**whites***
2 **slightly beaten egg yolks**	1 **cup whipping cream**
½ **cup sugar**	½ **cup chopped black**
¼ **teaspoon salt**	**walnuts or English**
1 **teaspoon vanilla**	**walnuts**

To caramelize sugar, in a heavy 8-inch skillet cook ½ cup sugar over medium-high heat until sugar begins to melt, shaking the skillet occasionally to heat the sugar evenly. Do not stir. Once the sugar starts to melt, reduce heat to low. Cook about 5 minutes more or until all of the sugar is melted and golden, stirring as needed with a wooden spoon. Slowly add the milk. Cook and stir over medium-low heat until the sugar is melted, stirring often.

In a medium saucepan gradually add the hot milk mixture to the egg yolks. Add ½ cup sugar and salt. Cook and stir over medium heat until mixture just coats a metal spoon. Remove pan from heat and stir in vanilla. Quickly cool the egg yolk mixture by placing the saucepan in a sink of ice water for 1 to 2 minutes, stirring constantly. Set aside.

Reconstitute dried egg whites according to package directions; beat with an electric mixer on high speed until stiff peaks form (tips stand straight). Whip cream until soft peaks form (tips curl over). Fold egg whites and whipped cream into cooled egg yolk mixture. Fold in the nuts. Pour into an 8×8×2-inch square baking pan. Cover; freeze for 1 hour. Stir; cover and freeze several hours or overnight or until firm. Makes 1½ pints.

Note: Eating eggs that have not been fully cooked is considered to be unsafe. Beaten egg whites should not be substituted for the dried egg whites. Look for this product in the baking section of the supermarket.

Nutrition facts per ½ cup: 393 calories, **24 g** total fat (**11 g** saturated fat), **131 mg** cholesterol, **148 mg** sodium, **40 g** carbohydrate, **0 g** fiber, **6 g** protein

If you love homemade ice cream but don't have an ice-cream freezer, this recipe is for you. The secret here is whipped dried egg whites* and cream folded into a caramel custard base. Amazingly, the black walnut-studded mixture is frozen in a baking pan (of all things!) and becomes ice cream with absolutely no churning.

1937 Strawberry Shortcake
Prep: 25 minutes   Bake: 15 minutes   Cool: 10 minutes

6 cups sliced fresh strawberries	½ cup butter
½ cup sugar	1 beaten egg
2 cups all-purpose flour	⅔ cup milk
2 teaspoons baking powder	1 cup whipping cream, whipped
	Fresh strawberries

Grease 8×1½-inch round baking pan; set aside. Mix sliced berries and ¼ cup of the sugar; set aside. Mix flour, baking powder, and remaining sugar. Cut in butter until mixture resembles coarse crumbs. Combine egg and milk; add to flour mixture. Stir just to moisten. Spread batter into prepared pan.

Bake in 450° oven for 15 to 18 minutes or until a toothpick comes out clean. Cool in pan 10 minutes. Remove from pan. Split into 2 layers. Spoon half of berry mixture and cream over first layer. Top with second layer, remaining berry mixture, and cream. Top with whole berries. Serve immediately. Serves 8.

Nutrition facts per serving: 307 calories, **13 g** total fat (**8 g** saturated fat), **59 mg** cholesterol, **227 mg** sodium, **44 g** carbohydrate, **3 g** fiber, **5 g** protein

Blueberry Rolls

Prep: 25 minutes   Bake: 20 minutes

1 16½-ounce can
    blueberries
1 recipe Rich Shortcake
    (see below)
1 tablespoon butter or
    margarine, melted
2 tablespoons sugar
½ teaspoon ground
    cinnamon

¼ cup sugar
2 tablespoons
    all-purpose flour
2 teaspoons lemon juice
    Vanilla ice cream
    (optional)

Drain blueberries, reserving juice; set aside. Grease a 2-quart square baking dish; set aside.

Prepare Rich Shortcake dough. On a lightly floured surface, roll dough into an 11×9-inch rectangle. Brush dough with melted butter or margarine. Combine the 2 tablespoons sugar and the cinnamon; sprinkle over dough. Sprinkle with 1 cup of the drained blueberries. Roll up, jelly-roll style, starting from a short side. Seal seam. Cut into 9 slices.

In a small saucepan combine the ¼ cup sugar and the flour. Add remaining blueberries and reserved juice. Cook and stir until thickened and bubbly. Remove from heat; stir in lemon juice. Pour blueberry mixture into prepared dish. Place rolls, cut sides down, on top of blueberry mixture. Bake in a 425° oven about 20 minutes or until rolls are golden brown. If desired, serve warm with vanilla ice cream. Makes 9 servings.

Rich Shortcake: In a medium mixing bowl combine 2 cups all-purpose flour, 4 teaspoons baking powder, 1 tablespoon sugar, and ½ teaspoon salt. Using a pastry blender, cut in ⅓ cup shortening until mixture resembles coarse crumbs. Make a well in the center of mixture. Add ⅔ cup milk and 1 beaten egg all at once. Stir just until dough clings together. On a heavily floured surface, coat the dough lightly with flour. Knead the dough gently for 10 to 12 strokes.

Nutrition facts per serving: 278 calories, **10 g** total fat (**3 g** saturated fat), **28 mg** cholesterol, **311 mg** sodium, **43 g** carbohydrate, **1 g** fiber, **4 g** protein

This luscious dessert is a cross between a blueberry shortcake and a blueberry cobbler. Spirals of rich shortcake dough, swirled with cinnamon-sugar, bake to a golden brown atop the blueberry sauce.

index